# Ancient Monuments
# in the United States

## E G Squier

ISBN (Print) 9781481932363

An ebook is available under the title
Ancient Archeological Sites in the Eastern United States
ISBN (ebook) 9781620600382

Folly Cove 01930
Gloucester MA


www.follycove.biz

# Table of Contents

# Part 1

Figure 1 - Mound on Tonnewanda Island, Niagra River

THE past half century, distinguished as it has been by activity and precision of research in the various departments of human inquiry, and fruitful as it has been in results, whether of discovery or demonstration, has been distinguished in no respect more than in the variety and importance of the illustrations which it has thrown upon the early history of men and nations. Through the devotion of individuals, and with the aids afforded by Governments and Societies, our geographical knowledge has not only been greatly extended, but the various families of humanity dispersed over the globe have been carefully studied, as well in their physical traits as in their mental and moral characteristics. Nor has inquiry satisfied itself with their present condition and aspects. Through the medium of their monuments and sculptured and painted or written records their past history has been elucidated, and the various phases of their progress or decline in arts, religion, and government deduced for the information and instruction of mankind.

The importance of what may be called the monumental element in these inquiries is well illustrated in the results which have followed on the researches of Champollion and his followers in Egypt, and of Rawlinson and Layard in ancient Assyria. Not only has a great deal that was uncertain in the fragmentary histories of ancient times been confirmed, but much that is new has been added, on the basis of evidence more conclusive and impartial than the testimony of historians. No account of the domestic life and the rites and ceremonials of the ancient Egyptians, however faithfully observed and recorded by contemporaries themselves, could convey to us the truth so clearly and accurately as the painted and sculptured walls of the ancient temples and tombs uncovered by Belzoni and Lepsius. Nor could even the glowing words of the prophets impress us with so direct and tangible evidence of the barbaric grandeur and power of the Assyrian monarchs as that which we obtain from the gigantic mythical figures, covered over with inscriptions, which have been dug up from the shapeless mounds of Asia Minor. How vivid become the descriptions of Herodotus, when we follow Pallas and Clarke in their explorations of the *tumuli* that dot over the plains of ancient Scythia! In them we find the golden corselet still resting on the breast of the ancient chieftain; his sword reduced to rust lies on one side, and the skeleton of his wife, the golden bracelets still circling her arms, are on the other, while at his feet moulder the bones of the steed which had carried him in life, and which was slain on his tomb.

Fortunately for the illustration of the condition of the arts and modes of life which existed in early times, and before man had achieved that high development of human intelligence, a written language, his religious conceptions were then such as to lead him to place in the tomb not only the personal ornaments, but the weapons and utensils of the deceased, and, in general, to raise over his remains a heap of earth or stones to mark and consecrate the spot. From these depositories, in many instances, have been drawn the only evidences of the existence of nations which disappeared, before the dawn of history, from countries now occupied by new or transplanted races; and it is equally from these that we derive, in other cases, the data on which to estimate the early condition of nations now proud, powerful, and civilized.

No department of history can be more exact than that which is based on the irrefutable evidences of these monuments. The British Islands afford us a marked and interesting example of their value. Not only have the successive races which lived there from the earliest times recorded their advent and occupation thus imperishably, but the vicissitudes of conquest and the furtive and partial occupations by invaders have been in like manner broadly impressed on the surface of the country. If every line of written history were blotted out, the succession of races, the periods of their domination, their affinities, their relative civilization, most of their arts, and many of their religious ideas and forms of worship, and the leading features of their social life could be accurately deduced from these remains, which, to the uneducated eye, are only meaningless heaps of earth or rough piles of stone. They tell us, as plainly as could the pages of written history, of the occupation and diffusion of the ancient Celts and Saxons; of the intrusions of the Danes and the Belgae; of the conquests of the Romans; and of the commercial visits of the Phoenicians.

And, as apart from their sepulchral memorials, men often erected other monuments, open temples and structures of various kinds, artfully contrived to shadow out their most abstract ideas and conceptions, before they had attained a knowledge of writing or even acquired forms of expression capable of conveying them to others for this reason, as well as for the light which they reflect on the arts, the customs, and beliefs of their authors, do the ancient monuments of all parts of the world claim the attention and enlist the interest of inquiring minds; and more especially when, as is the case with a large class of the remains found in our own country, they are the sole evidences of the former existence of a people, numerous and widely diffused, concerning whom History is mute, and whose very name is lost to Tradition itself. But the rigid rules which regulate philosophical research in other departments of human knowledge are no less applicable here than in respect to geology or the fixed sciences. Indeed, if severe criticism can be supposed to be requisite in one case more than another, it is when, from the popular nature of the subject, the temptations to exaggeration and mere speculation are strongest. How strong these have been is best shown by the vast amount that has been written, in the way of deduction, in respect to the ancient monuments of the United States, preceding the evidence of facts, and upon data often palpably erroneous, and almost always poorly authenticated. Thus it has happened that the rude earthworks found in the State of New York have been set down as of Tartar origin, while the more regular and imposing monuments of the Mississippi Valley have been variously claimed as evidences of Jewish, Scandinavian, and even of Hindoo occupation of the country.

5

By one, a series of Indian marks on a rock in New England has been taken as a Runic, by another as a Hebrew, and by a third as a Phoenician inscription; and by a fourth, if possible less critical than the others, the sculptured impressions of human feet in the limestone of the Mississippi Valley have been advanced as true fossils—tracks left by men who lived at a remote geological period, and were contemporaries of the trilobite!

Of late years, however, reveries of this kind have been generally discarded, and the investigation of our monuments conducted on more rational and scientific principles. They have been accurately surveyed and carefully excavated, on a scale sufficiently large to settle their general and essential characteristics, and, to a considerable degree, their purposes, if not their date and origin. Further investigations may give new and confirmatory details, perhaps remove some existing doubts; but they can not materially vary the conclusions which we are now enabled to draw concerning them from data of sufficient scope and authenticity.

It is well known that the aborigines of this continent, however uniform in those physiological features which go to determine the question of race, were broken up in many families, of widely different conditions, who have left as widely differing traces of their occupancy. In Central America they attained their highest development in the arts, and have left us many imposing monuments, in no degree inferior to those of India in their extent and in the skill in construction and elaboration of ornament which they display. In Mexico, where the qualified civilization which existed was rather reflected than of original growth, they have also left many monuments of vast proportions and no insignificant architectural pretensions, the types of which, however, are to be sought for further southward, if, indeed, many of them do not owe their origin to colonies from the same direction. In New Mexico, also, we find considerable remains, but rather of edifices corresponding with those which are now built, and the forms and character of which have been determined by circumstances which still exist, instead of the temples and palaces, the "high places" and altars of the southern and more civilized families of which I have spoken. New Mexico now forms part of the United States; but in speaking of the ancient monuments of the United States I wish to be understood only as referring to those found in the Valley of the Mississippi and between the

Alleghenies and the Atlantic Ocean.

Here we find great numbers, ruder, in some senses of the word, than even those of New Mexico, but of a generally higher type, more diverse in character, and indicating a more active and enterprising race as their builders. They are chiefly what may be called earthworks, although sometimes built of stone; and may be divided into three grand classes, viz., Works of Defense, Religious Structures, and Sepulchral Monuments. Connected with these, and inseparable from them in any consideration of the subject of our antiquities, are the various relics of art found with the dead in the mounds, or under such circumstances as to show that they pertained to their builders.

But it is not to be supposed that, in a territory so vast as that which I have indicated, we are to look for remains of antiquity of uniform character, or the works of a single people. Nor does it in any degree follow that they should be of the same date, however much they may seem to coincide in purpose. A wide distinction, sufficiently exact for all practical purposes, is, in fact, to be made between the remains found in the Valley of the Mississippi and those to the eastward of the Alleghenies. Not only are the former much more numerous, and of much larger dimensions than the latter, but they embrace several types which are not found in the Atlantic States, where all the works seem clearly referable to the simplest purposes of defense and sepulcher. In the Mississippi Valley, on the other hand, the most imposing structures are those which are of evident religious origin, and which, in their form and construction, combine the elements of the Mexican *teocalli*, or sacred places, and the terraced pyramids of Central America.

Some of the largest inclosures, involving most skill and labor in their erection, are also of religious design; while other works, most remarkable of all and most interesting, are of symbolical import— huge *relievos* on the face of the earth, shadowing forth the religious or abstract ideas of their builders. In the Atlantic States these are wholly wanting. Their absence alone would be sufficient ground for drawing a wide line of distinction between the two series of remains —at least, so far as regards their origin. Not that the few and scattered monuments to the eastward of the Alleghenies do not resemble many of those in the Mississippi Valley; on the contrary, they may be said to be almost identical with them, but only in the sense that the defensive works of all rude or primitive peoples, consisting of a simple embankment and ditch, must necessarily resemble each other; and a mound of earth heaped up over the dead in one place must, in external appearance at least, exactly coincide with a mound heaped up by different hands, but for a similar purpose, elsewhere. These are inevitable coincidences, but do not imply connections, nor even the remotest relationship, on the part of those who built them.

## Monuments of the Atlantic States.

What may be designated as the ancient monuments of the Atlantic States are scattered, at considerable intervals, all over the country from Maine to Florida; but they are most abundant in Western New York and Central Pennsylvania. As already intimated, they are of two kinds; first, simple mounds, generally, if not always, covering a large number of skeletons; and second, embankments of earth—in one or two instances, of stone—of varying height, and inclosing areas averaging from one to four acres, the largest not exceeding sixteen acres.

As regards the mounds, they are never of large size, seldom exceeding five feet, but in a few instances reaching ten feet in height, by from twenty-five to sixty feet in diameter at the base. They are less numerous than the inclosures, or works regarded as defensive. We have no account of any which have been found further north than New Hampshire. There is one on the northern shore of Ossipee Lake, in that State, which was originally ten feet high, from forty-five to fifty feet in diameter, and overgrown with heavy timber. A slight excavation was made in it a number of years ago, in the course of which three entire skeletons were found, accompanied by some tomahawks and coarse pottery. It seems to have been a general burial place, or to have been heaped up over a number of the dead, after a battle, in commemoration of the event and in honor of the slain. A similar mound formerly existed on St. Regis Island, in the St. Lawrence River, which was excavated by Colonel Hawkins, of the United States Boundary Commission, in 1818. It was found to contain a number of skeletons, fragments of pottery, and other rude relics of art. Still another, of which a view is given at the head of this article, is found on Tonnewanda Island, in Niagara River. It was originally fifteen feet high. Immediately under its apex, on the original surface of the earth, was discovered what appeared to have been a circle of stones, perhaps ten feet in diameter, within which were several heaps of bones, each comprising three or four skeletons. They were of individuals of all ages, and had evidently been deposited after the removal or decay of the flesh. Traces of fire were perceptible on the stones and around them. Other *tumuli,* of like character, have been found in the central and southern parts of New York and Pennsylvania; and Mr. Jefferson, in his "Notes on Virginia," has given an account of one on Ravenna River, in that State, which, although but forty feet broad at the base, and seven feet high, he estimated to contain a thousand human skeletons. Those near the surface seemed to have been deposited without order, while those near the base were disposed with a certain degree of regularity.

Further to the southward, in the States of South Carolina and Florida, mounds are found which closely resemble those of the Mississippi Valley in size and form, and which, no doubt, belong to the same general system with them. The builders of the monuments of that valley seem to have spread along the Gulf of Mexico, on the south, but there is no evidence that they reached any point higher than the banks of the Wateree River. The remains found in South Carolina and Florida, therefore, as well as those of the States bordering on the Gulf of Mexico, will come more appropriately under consideration in treating of the Monuments of the West.

The uniform occurrence of a considerable number of skeletons in the few mounds which are found to the eastward of the Alleghenies sufficiently indicates their purpose; and the character of the relics found in them identifies them as having been built by the Indian tribes found in occupation of the country. The practice, however, of erecting such monuments over the dead was by no means general among them. They are to be regarded as exceptional, and doubtless owe their origin to a custom common among many of the North America Indians of collecting together, at fixed intervals, the bones of their dead, and finally depositing them, with many and solemn ceremonies, in a common grave. They were sometimes heaped together, and covered with earth, forming mounds; but usually they were placed in pits or trenches in the earth, forming those extensive depositories familiar in many parts of New York and Canada under the name of "bone pits." This second burial, called by the early writers the "Festival of the Dead," took place at different but regular intervals among the different tribes. Charleroix tells us that with some it occurred every eight years, but with the Hurons and Iroquois every ten years. Full accounts of the ceremonies practiced on these occasions have been left us by Brabeuf, Charleroix, Creuxius, Bartram, and others, but they are too long to be copied here. The discovery of copper kettles, iron axes, gunbarrels, and other articles of European manufacture in some of these depositories proves that this practice of general burial was kept up after the Discovery, and to a comparatively late period.

A more interesting class of remains than these general sepulchers are the inclosures popularly known as "Indian forts." These are numerous in New York and Pennsylvania, and a few have been found in New England, Canada, and Virginia. It is to be observed of this class of works generally, that they are most frequent in districts remarkable for fertility of soil, abounding in fish and game, and possessing the greatest number of requisites for easy subsistence; in other words, where circumstances were most favorable for permanent establishments. In respect of position they have a great uniformity. Most of them occupy high bluff points, or headlands, scarped on two or more sides, and naturally easy of defense. When found on lower grounds, they are generally on some dry knoll or little hill in the midst of a swamp, or where a bend in some stream serves to lend security to the position. In nearly all cases they are in close proximity to an unfailing supply of water, near copious springs or running streams. Gateways opening to these are almost always visible, flanked sometimes by supplementary defenses. The embankments forming them are seldom more than four feet high, with an exterior ditch of equal depth, inclosing variable areas, depending much on the nature of the ground, of from one to sixteen acres.

One of the most regular of these works found in the Atlantic States, and which furthermore is distinguished as being built of stone, is situated on the right bank of the Winnipiseogee River, near the head of Little Bay, in the town of Sanbornton, New Hampshire. The accompanying plan (Figure 2) is from a sketch made in 1822. Since that period a great part of the stones have been removed, and the outlines of the work are no longer distinct. At the time of the first occupation of the country by the whites the walls were between three and four feet in height, and three feet in thickness, faced with stones regularly laid up outwardly, and filled in with clay, shells, gravel, etc., from the river and the shores of the bay. None of the stones were of great size, but such as could be lifted by a man without difficulty. The site of the work is nearly level, descending a little from the walls to the bank of the river. In front, for half a mile, the surface is quite even. When first discovered, oak trees of large size

11

were standing within the walls, where also were found great numbers of Indian ornaments, pipes of stone and clay, fragments of coarse pottery, and arrowheads and hatchets of stone. On a small island in the bay, and not far distant, many bones and other remains have been uncovered by the plow, leading to the inference that here was a considerable burial place.

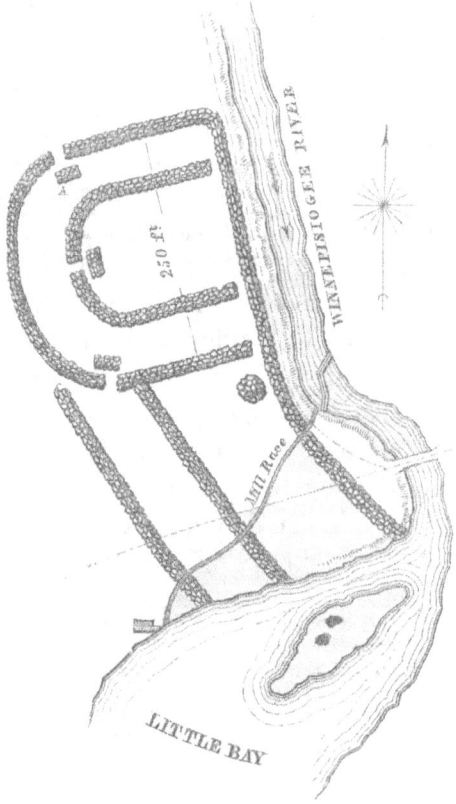

Figure 2 - Ancient Work in New Hampshire

It seems very evident that this work was erected for defense, and for keeping possession of the bay, which was a famous fishing place, and much frequented by the powerful tribe of the Penacooks, who, before their destruction by the Maquaas or Mohawks, sometimes mustered here as many as three hundred canoes at a single gathering. It certainly displays considerable skill in construction, and, if the walls were surmounted with palisades, would be almost impregnable under the system of warfare practiced by the Indians. The inner mounds, covering the entrances to the principal inclosure or citadel, form a feature peculiar to this work, and one not observed in any other now known to the eastward of the Alleghenies, among which it is furthermore unique in its regularity of form and in being built of stone. A similar work is said to have existed on the bluffs east of the Merrimack River, near Concord, on what was formerly known as "Sugar Ball Plain;" but no plan of it is in existence, and it is now too mach obliterated to be made out.

In New York the "Indian Forts," so far as known, consist uniformly of an earthen embankment, with an exterior ditch. Their numbers have been estimated at upward of a hundred, besides as many more which have been obliterated by the plow, or so much encroached upon as to be no longer satisfactorily traced. Not less than fifteen have been discovered in Jefferson County alone.

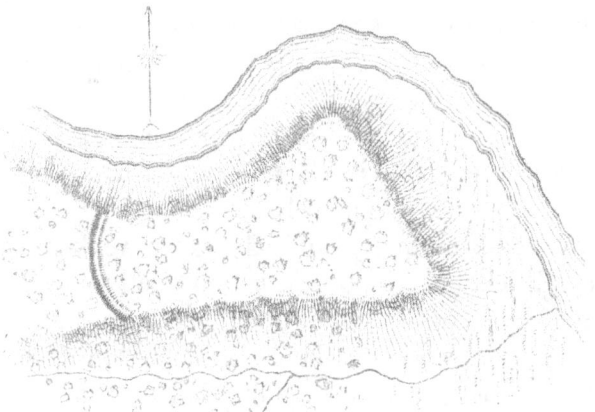

Figure 3 Ancient Work, Montgomery County, New York

A few examples, commencing with one found as far to the eastward as Montgomery County, will suffice to show their general character. (Figures 3 to 11.)

This work is situated on the right bank of Otstungo Creek, a branch of the Otsquago—itself a tributary of the Mohawk, about four miles in a southwestern direction from Fort Plain, in the town of Minden. It is known in the vicinity by the name of Indian Hill. The position is admirably chosen, and is, naturally strong and defensible. It is a high point of land projecting into a bend of the creek, which on one side has cut away the slate rock, so that it presents a mural front upward of one hundred feet in height, and entirely inaccessible.

13

Upon the opposite side is a ravine, within which flows a small stream. Here the slope, though not precipitous, is very abrupt; and if a line of palisades were carried along its brow, it would be entirely inaccessible to a savage assailant. Across the narrow isthmus which connects this headland with the adjacent high grounds is an embankment and ditch two hundred and forty feet in length, extending from the precipice upon the south to the brow of the ravine on the north, along which, curving inward, it is carried for some distance, terminating at a gigantic pine six feet in diameter. It has been supposed by some that this tree has grown up since the embankment was erected; but it seems most likely that it was the starting point of the ancient builders. The embankment is not of uniform height, but at the most elevated point rises perhaps six feet above the bottom of the ditch. No gateway is apparent, but one may have existed where a modern "wood road" crosses the intrenched line. The plan will afford an accurate idea of the position and its natural strength. The inclosed area is about seven hundred feet long by four hundred and fifty broad at its widest part, and contains very nearly six acres. It is densely covered with immense pines, throwing over it a deep gloom, and, with the murmur of the stream at the foot of the precipice, impressing the solitary visitor with feelings of awe, which the professed antiquary might deem it a weakness to acknowledge. Fragments of pottery and a variety of rude implements, as also copper kettles and other articles of European origin, have been found within the inclosure and in its immediate vicinity. Just outside of the wall a number of skeletons have been uncovered. They had been buried, according to the Indian custom, in a sitting posture. The valley of the Mohawk in this vicinity, it is well known, was the favorite seat of the tribe whose name it bears, and has been made classical ground by the stirring incidents of our early history. It was here the Indians maintained themselves until the period of the Revolution, and it seems probable that they erected the work in question at an earlier or later date in their history. It corresponds in position and character with the works in other parts of the State, and is precisely such a structure as we might expect to find erected by a very rude people.

Differing considerably from the work just described is that of which a plan is given on (Figure 4). It is situated a few miles to the eastward of the city of Buffalo, and derives much of its interest from

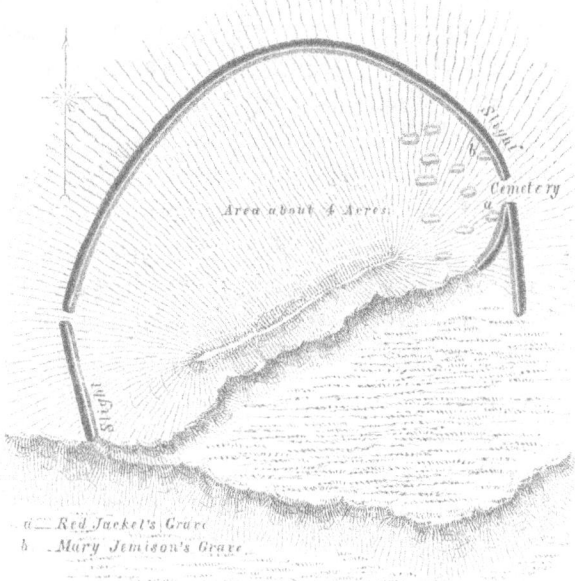

Figure 4 = Ancient Work Near Buffalo, New York

the associations connected with it. Within its walls lies buried the last and noblest of the proud and politic Iroquois, the haughty and unbending Red Jacket, who died exulting that the Great Spirit had made him an Indian. Here, too, rest the bones of Mary Jemison the "white woman," who was taken a prisoner by the Indians when a child, and afterward adopted their habits, became the wife of one of their chiefs, and remained with them until her death. The story of her life is one of the most eventful in our border history, full as it is of thrilling adventures and startling incidents.

The work is situated on the edge of a terrace or table land, moderately elevated above the low alluvions bordering Buffalo creek, at a point considerably higher than any other near it, and where the soil is sandy and dry. Assuming for it a defensive character, it will be seen that the terrace bank on one side is made to subserve the purposes for which the trench and embankments were constructed on the other. Although there is now no direct evidence to that effect, no doubt can be entertained that, in common with all the other works of the State, the wall was crowned with palisades, which were also carried along the brow of the terrace. The greater portion of this work has been for some time under cultivation; and the original lines are so much defaced that they would probably escape the notice of the careless observer. They may, nevertheless, be distinctly traced throughout their extent. At the point nearest the Indian cemetery, a portion of which is still spayed by the plow, the embankment is very distinct, and can not fail to attract attention. At a short distance to the northward of the work is a low spot of ground or marsh toward which opens a gateway. From this was probably obtained a portion of the supply of water required by the ancient occupants of the work. A number of springs start from the foot of the terrace, where the ground is also marshy. Within the walls of this work are to be found various traces of occupancy, such as the foundations of old lodges, fragments of pottery, etc. Tradition fixes upon this spot as the scene of the final and most bloody conflict between the Iroquois and the "Gah-kwas" or Eries—a tradition which has been supposed to derive some sanction from the fragments of decayed human bones which are scattered over the area. The old mission house and church stand in close proximity to this work. Red Jacket's house stood above a third of a mile to the southward upon the same elevation; and the abandoned council house still exists, perhaps a mile distant, in the direction of Buffalo. A little distance beyond the latter, in the same direction and near the public road, is a small mound, called "Dah-do-sot"— artificial hill— by the Indians, who, it is said, were accustomed to regard it with much veneration, supposing that it covered the victims slain in some bloody conflict in the olden time.

It was originally between five and six feet in height, by thirty-five or forty feet base, and is composed of the loam of the adjacent plain. A depression in the general surface of the ground is visible near it, marking the spot whence the earth for its construction was obtained.

Another work of similar character, and among those best preserved and most interesting, in the State of New York, overlooks the flourishing town of Auburn, in Cayuga County. It is situated on a considerable eminence, which rises abruptly from the level grounds on which the town is built to the height of perhaps one hundred feet. This is the most elevated spot in the vicinity, and commands a wide and very beautiful prospect. The ground occupied by the work subsides gently from the center of the area; but exterior to the walls are steep declivities and deep ravines, rendering approach in nearly every direction extremely difficult. These natural features are

Figure 5 - Ancient Work Near Auburn, New York

indicated in the plan, which obviates the necessity for a detailed description. Upon the south are several deep gulleys, separated by sharp, narrow ridges, rendering ascent at this point, in the face of determined defenders, entirely impracticable. It has been conjectured by some that the walls here have been washed away; but it is clear that there was slight necessity for any defenses at this point, and that none ever existed beyond what may still be traced. The number and relative proportions of the gateways or openings are correctly shown in the plan. That upon the north is one hundred and sixty feet wide, that upon the east sixty feet, and that upon the west thirty feet. These wide, unprotected spaces would seem to conflict with the supposition, so well sustained by its remaining features, that the work had a defensive origin. It is not improbable, however, that palisades extended across these openings, as well as crowned the embankments; for without such additions, as has been already observed, the best of these structures could have afforded but very slight protection. The embankments of this work are now between two and three feet in height, and the trenches of corresponding depth. The area of the work and the ground around it are covered with forest trees. There are several depressions, which, probably, were the caches of the ancient occupant *[The term cache, literally a hide or place of concealment, is of French origin, and has become*

17

*current among all the traders and trappers on the frontiers. The practice of caching, or hiding goods or provisions on outward marches, to be used upon returning, or by parties following, was derived from the Indians, among whom it was general A 'cache' is made by digging a hole in the ground, which is lined with sticks, grass, or any material which will protect the contents from the dampness of the earth. After the goods or provisions have been deposited the earth is carefully covered over, so as best to prevent the penetration of water from above. It is always necessary, at the least, to leave no signs by means of which rival parties or the cunning savages may discover the place of deposit. To this end the excavated earth is carried to a distance, and carefully concealed, or thrown into a stream, if one be near. Father Hennepin, in his account of his passage down the Mississippi River, in 1680, describes an operation of this kind in the following terms: "We took up the green sod, and laid it by, and digged a hole in the earth, where we put our goods, and covered them with pieces of timber and earth, and then put in again the green turf: so that it was impossible to suspect that any hole had been digged under it, for we flung the earth into the river."]*

Figure 6 View of Ancient Work Near Auburn, New York

It is said that a number of relics have been recovered here from time to time, and among others the head of a banner staff of thin iron, fourteen inches long and ten broad. It is, of course, of French or

18

English origin, and was probably lost or buried here by the Indians, into whose hands, by purchase or capture, it had fallen. We may, perhaps, refer it back to the days of Champlain and Frontenac, when the armies of France swept the shores of the Western lakes, in the vain hope of founding a Gallic empire in the New World. M'Cauley, in his History of New York, states that, in 1825, he examined the stump of a chestnut tree which stood in the ditch of this work, and counted the number of cortical rings or layers, marking the years of its growth. He found them to be 255 in number. As five years had elapsed since the tree had been cut down, this would carry back the date of the work certainly to 1565.. He found also the stump of another tree, three feet in diameter, standing in the ditch near by, which appeared to have fallen from decay, and which, in his opinion, dated as far back as the period of the Discovery. These facts certainly go far to give a high antiquity to the work in question; and it may well be, for aught that we know to the contrary, that several growths of forest intervened between the abandonment of the work and the date of the forest which now covers it.

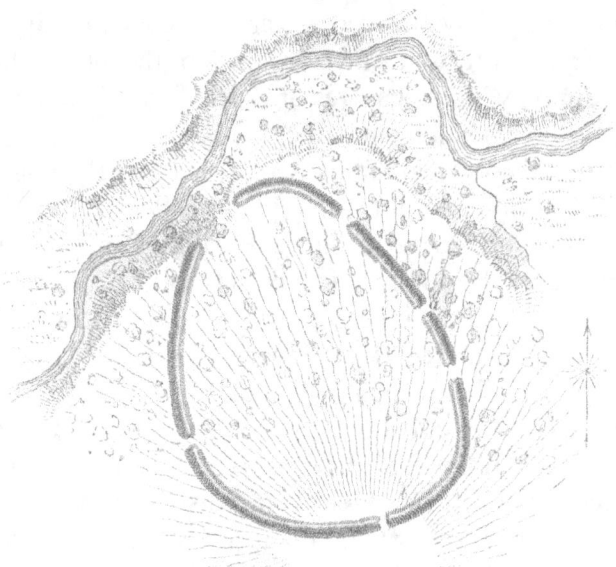

Figure 7 - Plan of Ancient Work Genessee County, New York

The work of which Figure 7 is a plan occurs in the town of Oakfield, Genessee County, half a mile west of the little village of Caryville. It is remarkable as being one of the best preserved and distinct of any in the State. It is situated upon the western slope of one of the billowy hills which characterize the rolling lands of the West, and between which the streams find their way to the rivers and lakes. The banks of the little stream which washes the work upon the north are steep, but not more than ten feet in height. Upon the brow of the bank, where the stream approaches nearest the work, the intrenchment is interrupted, and the slope toward the water is more gentle than elsewhere — indicating an artificial grade. The plan obviates the necessity for a detailed description. The embankments will now probably measure six feet in average height, calculating from the bottom of the trench. In the part of the work under cultivation it is easy to trace the ancient lodges. Here, too, is to be found the unfailing supply of broken pottery. At the sides of the principal gateway (a) leading into the inclosure from the east, according to the statement of an intelligent aged gentleman who was among the earliest settlers in this region, traces of oaken palisades were found, upon excavation, some thirty years ago. They were, of course, almost entirely decayed. A part of the area is still covered with the original forest, in which are trees of the largest dimensions. An oaken stump which measures upward of two feet in diameter stands upon the embankment at the point (b).

A mile to the northeast of this work was formerly a large inclosure, now entirely obliterated. It was called "Bone Fort" by the early settlers, from the circumstance that they found within it a mound six feet high and thirty feet broad, entirely made up of human bones slightly covered with earth. A few fragments of bones, scattered over the surface of the ground, are all that now mark the place of this sepulcher, which doubtless owed its origin to the aboriginal practice of collecting the bones of the dead, elsewhere referred to. Both of these works were perfect in 1788, when they were visited by Rev. Samuel Kirkland, Missionary to the Senecas, who has left an account of them in his journal. He says the place was called by the Senecas Tegataineáaghgue or "double fortified town," or a town with a fort at each end. He describes the one figured above as "inclosing about four acres of ground, and consisting of an embankment with a ditch from five to six feet deep. A small stream of water and a high bank," he continues, "circumscribes nearly the third of the inclosed ground. There are six gateway openings, and near the center a way dug to the water." This description, it will be observed, coincides closely with the plan, which is from the Survey made by myself in 1848.

Figure 8 - View of Ancient Work Genessee County, New York

Figure 9 - Ancient Work Erie County New York

Figure 9, which illustrates the class of lowland structures alluded to in the general remarks on the monuments of the Atlantic States, occurs about a mile distant from the village of Clarence, Erie County, New York. It is situated upon a sandy, slightly elevated peninsula, which projects into a low, tangled, and almost impassable swamp. A narrow isthmus or strip of dry ground connects it with the higher lands, which border the swamp on the south. It is small, containing less than an acre. The embankment does not preserve uniform dimensions, but has perhaps an average height of three feet. A mile to the eastward is another of the "bone pits" already several times referred to, which is estimated, by those who excavated it originally, to have contained four hundred skeletons heaped promiscuously together. They were of individuals of every age and sex. In the same field are found a great variety of Indian relics, also brass cap and belt plates, and other remains of European origin. Not far distant, some lime burners discovered, a year or two since, a skeleton surrounded by a quantity of rude ornaments. It had been placed in a cleft of the rock, the mouth of which was covered by a large stone.

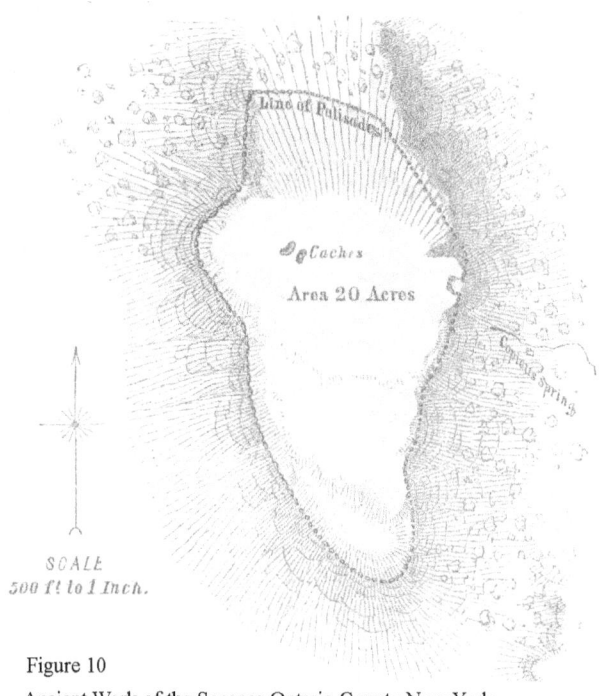

Figure 10

Ancient Work of the Senacas Ontario County New York

Examples of these works might be greatly multiplied, but those already adduced will be sufficient to illustrate their general character. Of those found in Pennsylvania we have no accurate plans, but the

22

descriptions of them given by observers show clearly that they differ, in no essential respect, from those of New York. In both States, however, there are other remains of works, unquestionably aboriginal, but of later date, which are worthy of notice from the light which they reflect on those already described. These are the remains of palisaded inclosures occupied by the Indians within the historical period, and the origin and objects of which are well known. An interesting example of this kind of works may still be traced in the town of Victor, Ontario County, New York, of which a plan is herewith given (Figure 10). Recent investigations have proved that the Marquis De Nonville penetrated here, in his famous expedition against the Senecas in 1687; and there is good reason for believing that the traces at present existing are those of the palisaded fort which was destroyed at that time. These traces consist of a narrow trench, formed in a stiff soil by the decay of the palisades or wooden posts planted in the ground, which constituted the defenses of the work.

This trench extends around and a little below the brow of a high hill, so steep on most sides as to be ascended only with the greatest difficulty. When in its perfect condition it must have been almost impregnable against the arms and attacks of savages. The sole entrance that can now be made out is at the point indicated on the right of the plan, where the palisades were carried for some distance inward, leaving an open rectangular space, which may have been occupied by a blockhouse or something equivalent. Nearly in front of this opening, and at the bottom of a deep and narrow ravine, a copious spring starts out from the hill. Within the inclosure are several deep holes, or excavations, by some called wells, but probably the caches in which the Indians kept their maize. In his letter of the 25th of August, 1687, De Nonville states:

"On the 14th July we marched to one of the large villages of the Senecas, where we encamped. We found it burned, and a fort near by quite abandoned; it was very advantageously situated on a hill......
We remained at the four Seneca villages for ten days. All the time was spent in destroying the corn, which was in such great abundance that the loss, including the old corn which was in cache, which we burned, was computed at 400,000 minots (equivalent to 1,200,000 bushels) of Indian corn."

The large village alluded to here is the one which was situated on the eminence now known as "Boughton,s Hill," not far from the work here figured, where abundant traces of Indian occupancy are found. These consist of copper kettles, French hatchets, broken gunbarrels, arrowheads, pipes, pottery, burned corn, etc. The iron recovered here at the time of the first settlement of the country was sufficiently abundant to repay the cost of clearing the grounds. Indeed it was the source whence the early blacksmiths, for a long distance around, derived the iron for ordinary consumption; and even now the smithies in the vicinity consume large quantities of the metal which the operations of agriculture continue to bring to light.

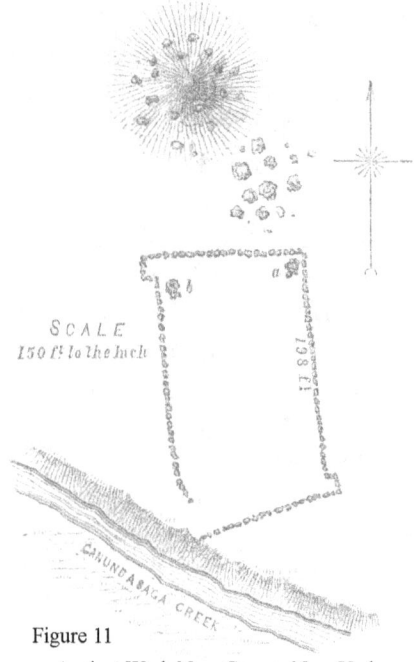

Figure 11

Ancient Work Near Geneva New York

Another palisaded work, but of more regular design and of later date, may still be traced in the neighborhood of the town of Geneva, in the same county with that above described. Its outlines are very distinct, and the holes left by the decay of the palisades may be traced with the greatest ease. Occupying level and accessible grounds, its preservation is entirely due to the circumstance that, at the time of the cession of their lands at this point, the Senecas made it a special condition that this spot should never be brought under

24

cultivation. "Here," said they, "sleep our fathers, and they can not rest well if they hear the plow of the white man above them." The stipulations made by the purchasers have been religiously observed. The site of this ancient palisade slopes gently toward a little stream called Ganundasaga Creek, which supplied the occupants of the fort with water. The ground is covered with a close green sward, and some of the apple trees planted by the Indians are still flourishing. In form the work was nearly rectangular, having small bastions at the northwestern and southeastern angles.

At (a) and (b) are small heaps of stone bearing traces of exposure to fire, which are probably the remains of forges or fireplaces. The holes formed by the decay of the pickets are now about a foot deep. A fragment of one of the pickets was removed in 1847, and is now in the State Cabinet at Albany. It is of oak.

A few paces to the northward of the old fort is a low mound with a broad base, and undoubtedly of artificial origin; it is now about six feet high, and is covered with depressions marking the graves of the dead. There is a tradition current among the Indians concerning this mound to the effect that a Seneca of giant proportions, having wandered west to the Mississippi, and from thence east again to the seacoast, about the period of the discovery of the country by Europeans, received a gun from a vessel, together with some ammunition, and an explanation of its use. Having returned to the Senecas at Ganundasaga, he exhibited to them the wonderful weapon, the first they had ever seen, and taught them how to use it. Soon after, from some mysterious cause, he was found dead, and this mound was raised over him on the place where he lay. It is averred by the Indians that, if the mound should be opened, a skeleton of extraordinary size would be found beneath it. It would be interesting, for a variety of reasons, to have this mound excavated. By whatever people erected, it is certain that it was extensively used by the Senecas for purposes of burial. In the cultivated fields surrounding the interesting work here described numerous relics have been discovered, chiefly, however, of European origin.

This fort was destroyed by General Sullivan in 1779. He burned the palisade, destroyed the crops in the adjoining fields, and cut down most of the fruit trees which the Indians had planted.

The foregoing examples illustrate sufficiently the general characteristics of the two classes of aboriginal remains found in the

Atlantic States, and go far toward identifying them as of a common origin, although possibly of different dates. They clearly coincide in position and purpose; and it seems evident that, for effective defense, the shallow ditches and low embankments of the earthworks would be wholly inadequate, unless the embankments were crowned with palisades. That such was the case is not only rationally inferable, but supported by direct and conclusive evidence. In the town of Elmira, Chemung County, there is a work closely corresponding with that found in Montgomery County, and already described. It is a high point of land, a bluff peninsula, washed on one side by the Chemung River, and protected on the other by a deep ravine with precipitous banks. Across the neck of land connecting it with the adjacent table or terrace, are carried two lines of ditches and embankments, the latter about three feet high and the former of corresponding depth. Running along the top, or crest, of each embankment is a depression resembling the furrow made by a plow. On careful examination, however, this is found to be a succession of holes left by the decay of the palisades which formerly surmounted the walls and constituted the real defenses of the position. It is only in tough and compact soils that such traces would be left for any great period of time; but here they remain, notwithstanding that large trees, and among them a yellow pine three feet in diameter, are standing on the embankments.

It may be objected that if the Indians found in occupation of the Atlantic States constructed earthworks of this kind, the fact could not have escaped the notice of the early explorers, and would have been made the subject of remark by them. The omission may be singular but is not unaccountable. They all speak of the aboriginal defenses as composed of palisades set in the ground. The simple circumstance of the earth having been heaped up around them to lend them greater firmness may have been regarded as so natural and simple an expedient as to be undeserving of a special mention, particularly as the embankment, in such a case, would be an entirely subordinate part of the structure. After the introduction of European implements, enabling the Indians to plant their pickets more firmly in the ground, and thus give them a strength before unattainable, the necessity for an embankment for that purpose became in a great degree obviated. We may thus account for its absence in their later structures, which also underwent some modifications of form suggested by the example or under the instructions of the whites, or by the new modes of warfare following on the introduction of firearms. Thus, in the plan of the old Seneca fort near Geneva, we find distinct traces of the bastion—a feature observable in none of the more ancient defenses.

It is true that the remnants of the Indian stock which still exist in New York generally profess total ignorance of the origin of the earthworks. But too much importance should not be attached to this circumstance. When we consider the extreme likelihood of the forgetfulness of ancient practices in the lapse of three hundred years, the absence of knowledge on this point is the weakest of all negative evidence, not to be weighed against the incontrovertible testimony of the works themselves.

As already said, the purposes for which they were erected are obvious. Their positions, general close proximity to water, and other circumstances not less conclusive, imply a defensive origin. The unequivocal traces of long occupancy found within many of them would further imply that they were fortified towns or villages, and were permanently occupied. Some of the smaller ones, on the other hand, seem to have been designed rather for temporary protection than permanent use—the citadels in which the builders sought safety for their old men, women, and children, in case of alarm or attack. The relics of art, and the traces of occupancy, found in them, it may be remarked further, are absolutely identical with those which mark the sites of towns and forts known to have been occupied by the Indians within the historical period. The pottery taken from these sites and from within the supposed ancient inclosures, is alike in all respects; the pipes and ornaments are indistinguishable; and the indications of aboriginal dwellings are precisely similar, and, so far as can be discovered, have equal claim to antiquity. Near many of these works are found cemeteries, in which well preserved skeletons are contained, and which, except in the absence of remains of European art, differ in no essential respect from the cemeteries found in connection with the abandoned modern towns and "castles" of the Indians.

In respect of the antiquity of these works nothing positive can be affirmed. Many of them are now covered with heavy forests; a circumstance upon which too much importance has been laid, and which in itself may not necessarily be regarded as indicative of great age, for we may plausibly suppose that it was not essential to the purposes of the builders that the forests should be removed. It is not uncommon to find trees of from one to three feet in diameter standing on the embankments and in the trenches, which would certainly carry back the date of their construction several hundred years, perhaps beyond the period of the Discovery in the fifteenth century. There is nothing, however, in this circumstance, nor in any other bearing upon the subject, which would necessarily imply that they were built by tribes anterior to those found in occupation of the country by the whites.

Indeed the weight of evidence is decidedly in favor of the conclusion that most of these works were erected by the Iroquois, or their western neighbors, and do not go back to a very high antiquity.

Their general occurrence upon a line parallel to and not far distant from the lakes, favors the hypothesis that they were built by frontier tribes —a hypothesis entirely conformable with aboriginal traditions. Here, according to these traditions, every foot of ground was contested between the Iroquois and the Gah-kwas and other western tribes; and here, as a consequence, where most exposed to attack, were permanent defenses most necessary. It was not until after their Confederation that the Five Nations were able to check and finally expel the warlike people which disputed with them the possession of this beautiful and fertile region; and it is not impossible that it was the pressure from this direction which led to that Confederation—an anomaly in the history of the aborigines. Common danger, rather than a far seeing policy, may possibly have been the impelling cause of the consolidation.

It follows from what has been adduced that, except in so far as they throw light on the system of defense practiced by the aboriginal inhabitants, and tend to show that they were to a degree fixed and agricultural in their habits, the aboriginal monuments of the Atlantic States have slight bearing upon the grand ethnological and archeological questions involved in the early history of this continent. The resemblances which they bear to the defensive structures of other rude nations, in various parts of the world, are the result of natural causes, and can not be taken to indicate either a close or remote connection or dependence. All primitive defenses, being designed to resist common modes of attack, are essentially the same in their principles, and seldom differ very much in their details. The aboriginal hunter and the semi-civilized Aztec selected precisely similar positions for their fortresses, and defended them upon the same general plan; yet it would be palpably unsafe to found conclusions as to the relations of the respective builders upon the narrow basis of these resemblances alone.

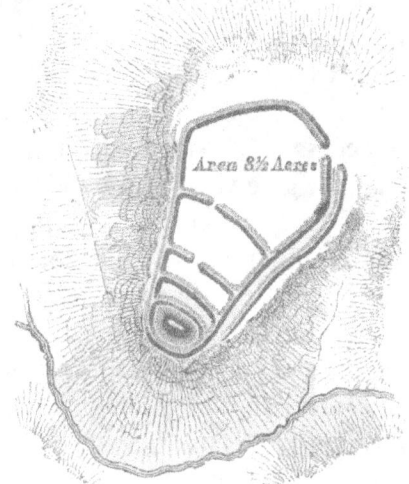

Figure 12 - Castle Comb, England

It has been hastily inferred, by many respectable authors who have written on the subject, that because certain monuments and aboriginal relics found in the United States, such as intrenched hills, *tumuli*, and instruments and ornaments of copper and stone, sustain analogies, in some instances amounting to identities, with those occurring in the British islands, and on the steppes of Tartary, that some connection must have existed between their makers and builders, or that they must have had a common origin. These resemblances are the inevitable results of similar conditions, and the ancient Celts and Scythians, the American Indians, and the rude islanders of the Pacific, built their hill forts, and fashioned their flint arrowheads and stone axes in like manner, because they thus accomplished common objects in the simplest and Most obvious manner. In the choice of their military positions the ancient Britons were governed by the same considerations with the builders of the works which we have noticed—advantage in all cases being taken of the natural features of the country. Their defenses were usually built on headlands, a single wall being carried around the brow of the promontory, while the level approaches were protected by a succession of embankments and ditches, with occasional advanced posts or outworks. In some instances steep isolated hills were selected, which were defended by a series of concentric embankments, carried around their summits. The subjoined plan (Figure 12) from Sir R. C. Hoare's "Ancient Wiltshire," will illustrate the general character of these works. It is found in the neighborhood of Castle Combe, from which it takes its name, and is placed on the point of a very steep hill, at the base of which flows a rapid stream. It is very difficult of access on all sides except one, in which direction there is a narrow gateway. It contains eight and a half acres. The defenses consist of an embankment extending entirely around the brow of the hill or promontory, which is doubled on the right, where the natural declivity is least and cagiest to be scaled. Entering the inclosure from the north, the explorer encounters three lines of ramparts, intersecting its area, through two of which are openings. The third completely shuts in a high mound, which commands the whole area, and which seems to have been designed as a citadel or place of last resort, in case the outer works were forced by an enemy.

Taking this as a fair example of ancient British defenses, we perceive that in position and mode of construction they are indistinguishable from those of our own country already described. They might be regarded, so far as their apparent features are concerned, as the works of the same people; yet they were constructed by different races, separated from each other by ocean wastes, and having little in common, except the possession of those savage passions which have reddened every page of the world's history with blood. They serve only further to illustrate how naturally, and almost of necessity, men similarly circumstanced hit upon common methods of meeting their wants; but they do not necessarily establish a common origin, nor a constant nor casual intercourse.

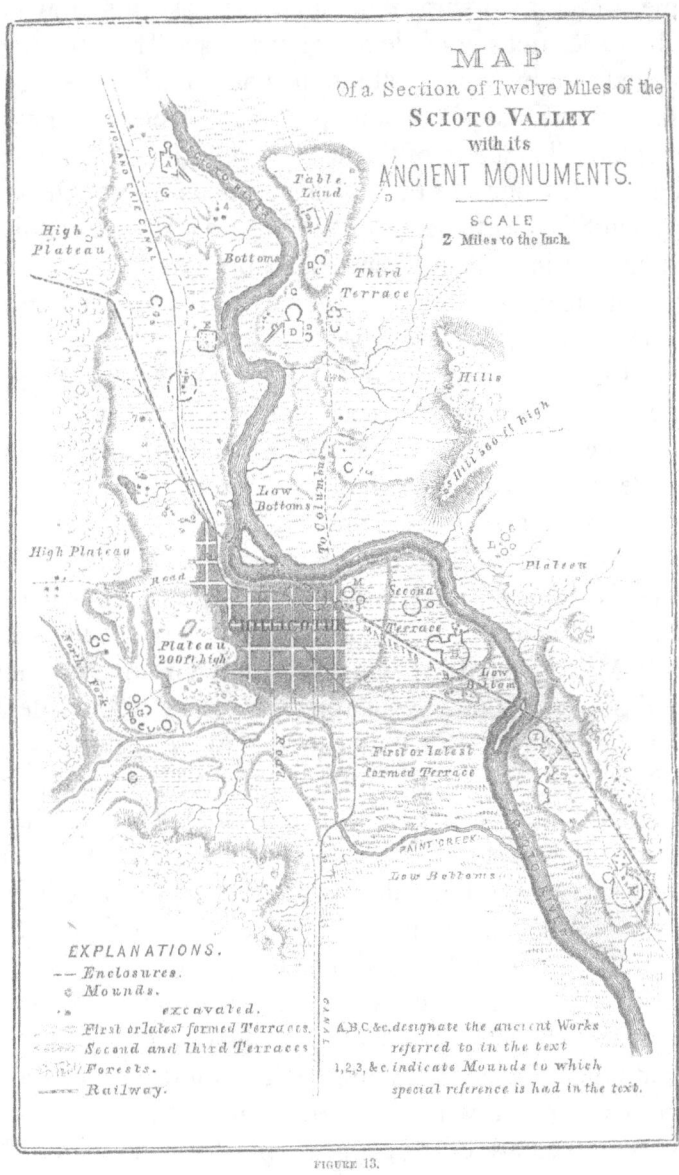

FIGURE 13.

The small, rude, and scattered monuments of aboriginal labor and skill found to the eastward of the Allegheny Mountains, and which I have just described, give place, in the Valley of the Mississippi

31

River, to numerous large and skillfully constructed works, not alone of defense, but connected with the religious notions and systems of their builders; vast open temples in which they performed the ceremonies of their worship, and high places or altars on which they offered their sacrifices or made their adorations. They are accompanied also by sepulchral mounds or *tumuli*, covering the ashes of chieftains and priests, and perhaps reflecting in their size the relative rank or distinction of the dead. In addition to these, there are found huge representations of men and animals, chiefly, however, in Wisconsin and the Northwest, constituting vast *relievos* on the face of the country or in some instances probably symbolical in design, but on the whole enigmatical and anomalous. In these mounds, and in such connection with these works as to justify the belief that they owe their origin to a common source, have been found many minor relics of art in stone and metal, sculptures curiously and often skillfully and elaborately wrought, and instruments and ornaments of materials derived from unknown or distant localities.

These various classes of remains are spread over a very wide extent of country. They are found in great numbers in Ohio, Indiana, Illinois, Wisconsin, Missouri, Arkansas, Kentucky, Louisiana, Mississippi, Alabama, Georgia, and Florida. They occur in less numbers in Michigan, Alleghania or Western Virginia, in Minnesota, Texas, and South Carolina. None (except perhaps a few defensive works coinciding in origin with those of New York and Pennsylvania) are found to the northward of the great lakes; but in the Mississippi Valley Carver discovered some of them as high as Lake Pepin, and Lewis and Clark found a considerable work on the Missouri River, a thousand miles westward from its mouth. It is by no means to be understood that they are equally distributed over this wide area; they are generally confined to the valleys of the rivers and large streams, and rarely occur in the broken or back country, away from the water. They are almost always found, furthermore, in districts and places where the soil is rich and fertile, and where fish and game were probably most abundant. In all these respects they fully justify the remark of the geographer Flint, who says: "The most dense ancient populations existed in precisely the places where the most crowded populations will exist in ages to come. The appearance of a series of mounds generally indicates the contiguity of rich and level lands, easy communications, fish, game, and the most favorable adjacent positions." Indeed, the sites selected for settlements, and which have been found most favorable for the establishment of towns by our own people, are often those which were the principal seats of the mound builders, and where they have left most traces of their occupancy. Marietta, Newark, Portsmouth, Chillicothe, Circleville, and Cincinnati in Ohio, Frankfort in Kentucky, and St. Louis in Missouri, all stand on the sites of extensive ancient works which have in some instances determined the plans of the existing cities.

And although it may be observed of these remains that, with the exception of the animal shaped effigies of Wisconsin, they are all of one general type, yet the relative number of works palpably defensive, and of inclosures and *tumuli* manifestly religious, varies very materially in the different parts of the field of their occurrence. Defensive works are abundant in Ohio and Kentucky, and are comparatively rare in the more Southern and Western States. The regular inclosures, which, for reasons adduced further on, are regarded as of religious origin, are also most numerous in the States above named; while, on the other hand, the regular mounds, truncated and terraced pyramids, and structures coinciding in type with the *teocallis* of Mexico, become larger and more numerous as we descend the Mississippi River and approach the Gulf of Mexico. The greater number of defensive works to the northward may be accounted for, hypothetically, by assuming that the mound builders were pressed upon by hostile neighbors from that direction; and we may regard the more regular and systematic works, further to the southward, as due to a less disturbed and more developed condition of the people who built them. Deductions of this kind, however, will be more appropriate after we have considered the monuments under notice in detail, as well in reference to their peculiarities as in respect of their geographical positions.

As regards the number of these ancient monuments nothing, can be affirmed with exactness; it is, however, very great. In the State of Ohio alone it has been calculated, on very good data, that there are not less than ten thousand *tumuli* or mounds, and from one thousand to fifteen hundred inclosures of various sizes. Some notion may be formed of their abundance and distribution from the map preceding, showing "A section of twelve miles of the valley of the Scioto River, in Ohio." Within this area, it will be observed, there occur upward of

Figure 14 The Great Mound Near Miamisburgh Ohio

one hundred mounds, some of them of large size, and not far from forty inclosures of all classes. Some of these, like those designated by the letters (K), (H), and (D), have embankments between two and three miles in circuit. Indeed the magnitude of a large part of these remains is not less remarkable than their great numbers. Lines of embankment, varying in height from five to thirty feet, and inclosing areas of from one to fifty acres are common; while inclosures of one and two hundred acres area are far from infrequent. Occasional works are found embracing as many as four hundred acres. The magnitude of the area which they inclose, however, is not always a correct index of the amount of labor which they have cost. A fortified hill in Highland County, Ohio, has one mile and five-eighths of heavy embankment, yet it incloses an area of only about forty acres. A similar work on the Little Miami River, in Warren County in the same State, has upward of four miles of embankment; yet it incloses but little more than one hundred acres. A group of works on the Ohio River at Portsmouth, near the confluence of the Scioto River with that stream, has an aggregate of at least twenty miles of embankment; yet the entire amount of land embraced within the walls does not probably much exceed two hundred acres.

The mounds are as variable in dimensions as the inclosures themselves, and range from such as are but a few feet in height, and a few yards in diameter, to those which, like the Grave Creek mound in Virginia, rise to the height of seventy feet, and measure a thousand feet in circumference at their base. A large conical mound in the vicinity of Miamisburgh, in Ohio, measures sixty-eight feet in vertical height, and eight hundred and fifty-two in circumference at its base, and contains 311,353 cubic feet. Of still greater dimensions is the quadrangular truncated mound of Cahokia, Illinois, opposite and almost within sight of St. Louis. It has an altitude of ninety feet, and is upward of two thousand feet around at its base, containing, on a rough calculation, 20,000,000 cubic feet of earth. Another great mound near Selsertown, Mississippi, is computed to cover six acres of ground. As already observed, mounds of these extraordinary dimensions are most common in the Southern States. The usual dimensions of this class of ancient remains, however, are much less than in the examples above given. The greater number range from six to thirty feet in perpendicular height, by from forty to one hundred feet in diameter at the base.

Figure 15 The Great Mound of Cahokia Illinois

In view of their great numbers, and the large size of many of them, persons have not been wanting to suggest that they are natural formations, "the results of diluvial action," modified in some instances but never erected by man. But the suggestion could never have been made by any person who had enjoyed the opportunity of seeing and examining them for himself. They are uniformly so placed in reference to the adjacent country, and their conformation is so distinct and peculiar, that the eye can not long hesitate in recognizing them. Their contents, moreover, establish their artificial origin beyond dispute or question.

In respect of form, it may be observed that a large, perhaps the larger part of the inclosures are regular in outline, the circle predominating. Some are squares, some parallelograms, others are ellipses or polygons, regular or irregular. The regular works almost invariably occur on level grounds, care evidently having been taken by their builders to select those smoothest and least cut up by ravines or water courses. The irregular works are those which partake most of the character of defenses, and are usually made to conform to the nature of the ground on which they are erected. They rim around the brows of hills, across the isthmuses of peninsulas which are protected on other sides by streams or steep and inaccessible precipices, and vary in the height of their walls and the depth of their ditches with the naturally greater or inferior strength of the point protected. The square and the circle often occur in combination, frequently communicating with each other directly, or by avenues consisting of parallel lines of embankment. Detached parallels are by no means rare, and are perhaps among the least explicable of all the ancient monuments.

Figure 16 Mound and Circle Near Blennerhassett's Island, Virginia

The mounds are usually simple cones in form; but they are sometimes truncated, and occasionally terraced with graded or winding ascents to their summits. Most are circular; but some are elliptical, others pear shaped, and others squares or parallelograms, with aprons or terraces and graded ascents. Besides these, there are others already alluded to, most frequent in Wisconsin and the Northwest, which take the form of animals and reptiles. Another variety of remains are elevated causeways, sometimes called "roads," and graded descents, or "covered ways," to rivers and streams, or from one terrace to another.

As already remarked, these works occur mainly in the valleys of the Western rivers. The alluvial terraces by which these valleys are marked, known locally, and perhaps accurately, as "river bottoms," were the favorite sites of the mound builders. The principal monuments are found where these "bottoms" are most extensive —at the junction of streams, or where the valleys are broadest and most favorable for their erection. The works at Marietta, at the junction of the Muskingum and Ohio rivers; at the mouth of Grave Creek; at Portsmouth, the junction of the Scioto with the Ohio; and at the mouth of the Great Miami, are examples in point. Occasional works are found on hilltops, or on headlands overlooking valleys, or at little distance from them; but these are manifestly, in most instances, works of defense, or of resort against enemies, or in some way connected with warlike purposes.

In the next part we shall consider the works thus generally described in detail, and illustrate fully their features and probable purposes.

# Part 2

2-1 View of Hopeton Works, Ohio

IN a preceding article I have given a general and rapid outline of the ancient monuments of the Mississippi Valley, from which it will be seen that they resolve themselves into several well defined classes, which should be treated of in the order of their importance and dependence. To this end the following classification will probably prove sufficiently exact and convenient:

I. Inclosures for defense.
II. Sacred Inclosures.
III. Sepulchral Mounds.
IV. Sacred, Alter or Temple Mounds.
V. Animal Shaped Mounds.
VI. Mounds of Observation.
VII. Implements and Utensils.
VII Ornaments.

In the present paper I shall treat of the first two of the above classes, leaving the other for a subsequent and concluding article.

## Inclosures for Defense

[Often of vast size; occupying elevated, commanding, or defensible positions; irregular in outline, conforming in this respect to the nature of the ground; ditch usually exterior to the walls; embankment usually double or treble; entrances often intricate, and defended by traverses and horn works; often have sentinel mounds or lookouts, and natural springs or artificial reservoirs within their walls, occasionally built of stone.]

Those works which are incontestably defensive always occupy strong natural positions. To understand their character and capacity for the purpose assigned to them we must consider the predominant features of the country in which they occur. The Valley of the Mississippi, from the base of the Alleghenies to the ranges of the Rocky Mountains, is a vast sedimentary basin, and owes its general aspect to the powerful action of water. Its rivers have worn their valleys deep in a vast original plain, leaving in their gradual subsidence broad terraces, marking the different eras of their history. The edges of the table lands, bordering on the valleys, are cut by a thousand ravines, presenting bluff headlands and high hills with level summits, sometimes connected by narrow isthmuses with the original table, and sometimes entirely detached. The sides of these elevations are always steep and difficult of ascent, in some cases precipitous and absolutely inaccessible. The natural strength of such positions, and their susceptibility of defense, would certainly suggest them as the citadels of a rude people having hostile neighbors or pressed by foreign invaders. Accordingly, we are not surprised at often finding these heights occupied by strong and complicated works, the design of which is indicated no less by their position than by their peculiarities of construction. In such cases it is always to be observed that great care has been exercised in their selection, and that they possess peculiar strength and adaptation for the purposes to which they were applied. While rugged and steep on most sides, they have one or more points of comparatively easy approach, in the protection of which the utmost skill of the builders has been expended. They are guarded by double, overlapping walls, or a series of them, having sometimes an accompanying mound, designed perhaps as a "lookout," and corresponding to the barbican in the system of defense of the Middle Ages. The usual defense is a simple parapet thrown up along and a little below the brow of the hill, varying in height and solidity as the declivity is more or less steep and difficult of access.

Other defensive works occupy the peninsulas formed by the streams, or cut off the bluff points formed by their junction with each other. In such cases a fosse and wall are carried across the isthmus, or diagonally from the bank of one stream to that of the other. In certain instances the wall is double, and extends along the bank of the stream for some distance inwardly, as if designed to prevent an enemy from turning the flank of the defense.

To understand clearly the nature of the works last mentioned, it should be remembered that the banks of the Western rivers are always steep, and where these works are situated invariably high. The banks of the various terraces are also steep, ranging from ten to thirty feet and upward in height. The rivers are constantly shifting their channels, and frequently cut their way through all the intermediate up to the earliest formed or highest terrace, presenting bold banks from fifty to one hundred feet high. At such points, from which the rivers have receded to the distance of half a mile or more, works of this description are oftenest found.

These preliminary remarks will serve to introduce examples of the various kinds of defensive structures alluded to, and which will illustrate the characteristics pointed out in the classification. Figure 2 is an accurate plan of a remarkable stone work, which occupies the summit of a lofty, detached hill, twelve miles westward from the city of Chilicothe, Ohio, near the village of Bourneville. The hill is not far from 400 feet high, and remarkable for the abruptness of its declivities, which, in places, are absolutely inaccessible. This promontory is the advance point of a range of hills situated between the narrow valleys of two small streams, and projects boldly into the broad valley of Paint Creek, so as to constitute its most prominent natural feature. Its summit is a level and fertile area, with some considerable depressions, which receive and retain the water collected from rains for the entire year.

The defenses consist of a wall of stones, which is carried around the hill a little below its brow; but in some places it rises to the general level of the summit, so as to cut off projecting spurs of the hill, and is furthermore carried across the neck of land or isthmus which connects the hill with the table land behind. By the term wall

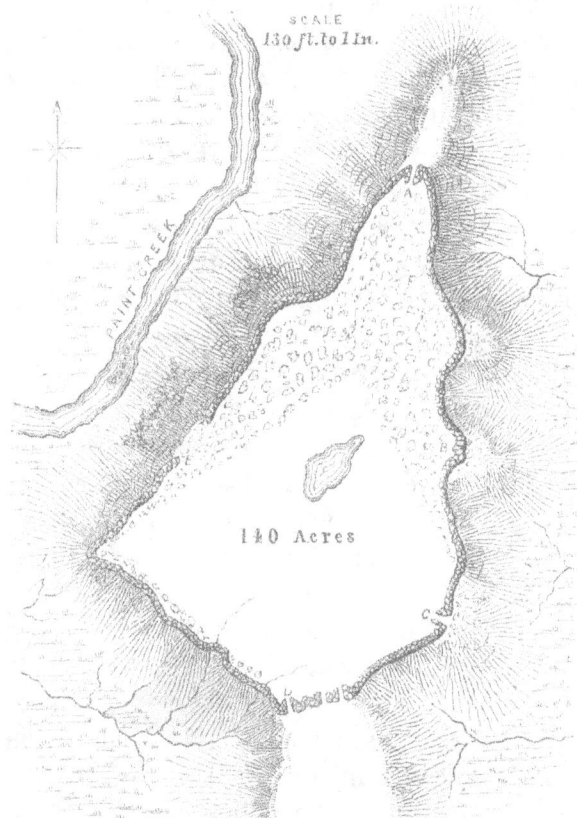

Figure 2-2 Stone Work in Valley Of Paint Creek, Ohio

must not be understood a wall of stones laid up with regularity, as in a modern fortification, but rather a line of stones heaped together, with but faint evidences of artificial arrangement, and best described as presenting the appearance which might be expected from the falling outward and downward of a wall of stones placed, as this was, on the declivity of a hill. On the western, or steepest face of the hill, the stones have slipped down, in the course of time, so as to cover a line from thirty to fifty feet broad, and resemble the "retaining walls" of our railways and canals. But for the amount of stones it might be taken for a natural feature —the debris of the outcropping sandstone strata. But this impression would be speedily corrected on reaching the points where the supposed line of debris, rising over the spurs of the hill, forms a series of gateways, and then

41

subsides and resumes its course as before.

On the eastern face of the hill, where the declivity is least abrupt, the wall is heaviest, and from fifteen to twenty feet base, by from three to four feet in height. Where it crosses the istmus, at (D), it is heavier still; and although stones enough to build a stout division wall between two proprietors have been removed from it, yet the diminution is not discernible. This isthmus is 700 feet across, and the wall is carried across it, in a right line, at its narrowest point. Here are three gateways opening into the work from the continuous terrace beyond. These were formed by curving the ends of the walls inward for forty or fifty feet, leaving narrow passages between, not exceeding eight feet in width. At other points, indicated in the plan by the letters (A) and (C), where there are jutting spurs or ridges from the main body of the hill, are similar gateways. It is at these points that the hill is most easy of access. At (B) seems to have been a similar gateway, which, for some reason, was closed up. A like feature may be observed in the line of wall at (D). At these gateways the amount of stones is more than quadruple the quantity at other points, constituting broad, mound shaped heaps. They exhibit strong marks of fire, which in some specimens has vitrified their surfaces and fused them together. Light, porous, scoriaceous material is also abundant in the centers of some of these piles. Indeed, the evidences of great heat are visible at many places on the line of the wall, particularly at (F), the point commanding the widest expanse of country. Here are two or three small mounds of stone, which appear to have been burned throughout. Nothing can be more certain than that powerful fires were maintained, for considerable periods, at numerous prominent points on the hill; for what purposes, except as alarm signals—"fire towers"—it is impossible to conjecture.

It will be observed that at (E), where the hill is precipitous and inaccessible, the wall, elsewhere continuous, is interrupted, evidently because none was needed there for purposes of protection. There are also, as has already been remarked, several depressions on the hill, possibly artificial, which retain a constant supply of water—an indispensable requisite in a fortified work designed to resist a prolonged assault. One of these covers about two acres, and furnishes a supply of water estimated by the proprietor of the hill, who resides near the reservoir, as sufficient for the wants of a thousand head of cattle.

The area of this singular work is something over one hundred and forty acres, and the line of wall is upward of two miles and a quarter in length. Most of the works, and a large portion of the area, are still covered with a primitive forest. Trees of the largest size grow on the wall, twisting their roots among the stones, some of which are firmly imbedded in their trunks. That this work was designed for defense will not admit of doubt. The wall was probably once regularly laid up, and, if it does not now present any clear evidence of that having been the case, we must consider that it was built on a yielding and disintegrating declivity, and that successive forests in their growth and prostration, aided by the action of the elements, would have been adequate to the total ruin of structures much more solid and substantial than we are justified in supposing any of the stone works of the mound builders to have been. The stones, it may be added, are uncut, of all sizes, and probably sufficient to have constructed a wall eight feet high and of equal thickness. It can readily be perceived that, on a steep declivity such as this hill presents on every side, so large an amount of stones, even though simply heaped together, must have proved a serious impediment in the way of an assailant, especially if crowned by a line of palisades.

In the magnitude of area inclosed, this work exceeds that of any other hill work now known in the United States; but the wall is considerably less in length than that of the hill work popularly known as "Fort Ancient" on the Little Miami River, thirty-five miles above Cincinnati. The valley which it overlooks was a favorite spot with the mound builders, who have left in it numerous mounds of large size, and several extensive works, of the class denominated Sacred Inclosures. It is the only work of a defensive character within a radius of many miles; and we may not unreasonably infer, from its large size, and the amount of labor expended on it, that it was the citadel or place of last resort of a large, and fixed, and therefore agricultural population, surrounded by hostile neighbors, or liable to sudden irruptions from abroad.

It may be observed here that works of stone are very rare, not more than three or four having fallen under the notice of the writer in the whole course of his investigations. Figure 3, therefore, may be taken as a better type of the "Hill Forts" or defensive inclosures than the work last described. It is situated in Butler County, Ohio, on the west side of the Great Miami River, about three miles below the

43

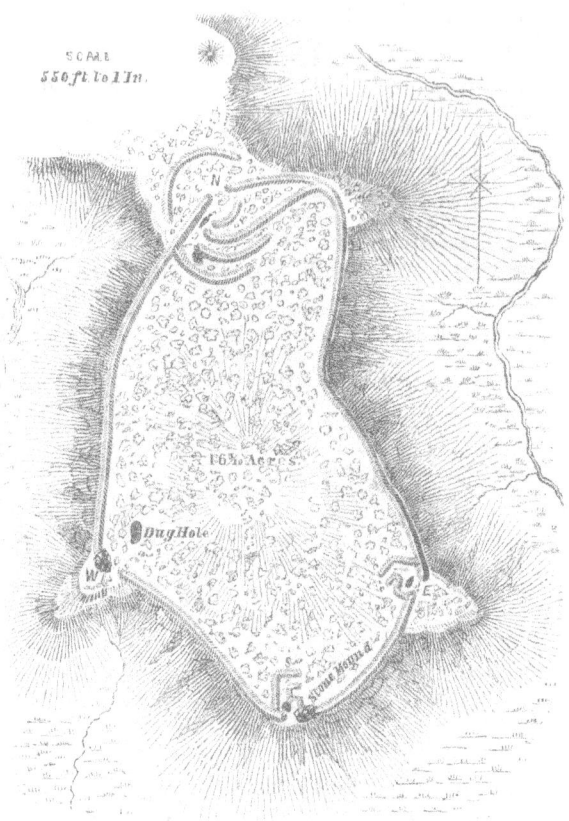

2-3 Fortified Hill Butler County Ohio

town of Hamilton. It illustrates, in a special manner, some of the most interesting features of this class of works, and on that account merits a particular description. The hill itself is half a mile distant from the present bed of the river, and is not far from two hundred and fifty feet high, being considerably more elevated than any other in the vicinity. It is surrounded at all points, except a narrow space toward the north, by deep ravines, presenting steep and almost inaccessible declivities. The slope toward the north is very gradual, and from that direction the hill is easy of approach. It is covered by a primitive forest.

Skirting the brow of the hill, and generally conforming to its outline, is a wall of mingled earth and stone, having an average height of five feet by thirty-five base. It has no apparent ditch, the earth composing it, which is a stiff clay, having been for the most

44

part taken up from the surface, without leaving any marked excavations. There are a number of pits or "dug holes," however, at various points within the walls, from which it is evident a portion of the material was obtained. The wall is interrupted by four openings or gateways, each about twenty feet wide; one fronting the north, on the approach above mentioned, and the others occurring where the spurs of the hill are cut off by the parapet, and where the declivity is least abrupt. They are all, with one exception, protected by inner lines of embankment of a most singular and intricate description. These are accurately delineated in the plan, which will best explain their character. It will be observed that the northern or great gateway, in addition to its inner maze of walls, has an outwork of crescent shape, the ends of which approach within a short distance of the brow of the hill.

The excavations are near the gateways: none of them are more than sixty feet over, nor have they any considerable depth. Nevertheless they all, with the exception of the one nearest to gateway (S), contain water for the greater portion if not the whole of the year. A pole may be thrust eight or ten feet into the soft mud at the bottom of those at (E).

At (S) and (H), terminating the parapet, are mounds of stones, thrown loosely together, eight feet in height. Thirty rods distant from gateway (N), and exterior to the work, is a mound ten feet high, on which trees of the largest size are growing. It was partially excavated a number of years ago, and a quantity of stones taken out, all of which seemed to have undergone the action of fire. The ground in the interior of the work gradually rises, as indicated in the section, to the height of twenty-six feet above the base of the wall, and overlooks the entire adjacent country. In the vicinity of this work are a number of others occupying the valley—no less than six, of large size, occurring within a distance of six miles down the river.

The character of this structure is too obvious to admit of doubt. The position which it occupies is naturally strong, and no mean degree of skill is employed in its artificial defenses. Every accessible avenue is strongly guarded. The principal approach, the only point of easy access, or capable of successful assault, is rendered doubly secure. A mound, used perhaps as an alarm post, is placed at a short distance in advance, and a crescent wall crosses the isthmus, leaving but narrow passages between its ends and the steeps on either hand.

45

Next comes the principal wall of the inclosure. In event of an attack, even though both these defenses were forced, there still remained a series of walls so complicated as inevitably to distract and bewilder the assailants, thus giving a marked advantage to the defenders. This advantage may have been regarded as more considerable than we, in our ignorance of the military system of the ancient people, would suppose. From the manifest judgment with which their military positions were chosen, as well as from the character of their intrenchments, so far as we understand them, it is safe to conclude that all parts of this work were the best calculated to secure the objects of the builders under the modes of attack and defense then practiced. On the assumption that the embankments were crowned with palisades, it is easy to believe that it afforded entire security against rude or savage foes.

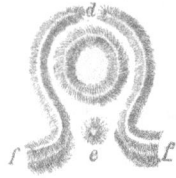

2-4 Plan of Entrance

The devices resorted to in this work for protecting the principal entrances to it are repeated with slight modifications in other works, and are found also in some of the military structures of the Mexicans. Figure 4 is a plan of the great entrance to a defensive work, in the same valley with that above described, seven miles distant to the northward. As they approach each other, on either side, the walls curve inwardly, on a radius of seventy-five feet, forming a true circle interrupted only by the gateways. Within the area thus formed, is a small, complete circle, one hundred feet in diameter; outside of which, and covering the gateway, is a mound, (e), forty feet in diameter and five feet high. The passage between the mound and embankment on each side is about six feet wide. The gateway, or opening, is twenty feet wide. The letters (f f) indicate the fosse or ditch which surrounds the work, but which is interrupted at the entrance. The wall which Cortez encountered in his march on the city of Mexico, covering the eastern approach to the Tlascallan territories, is described by Bernal Diaz as six miles long, with an entrance formed by the ends lapping round on each other in the form of semicircles having a common centre. And De Bry, in describing the defenses of the Floridian Indians, affirms that they were constructed of palisades, which "at the entrance were drawn in, after the fashion of a snail's shell." Similar devices were resorted to by the Romans, in their *castra stativa* or field forts, as shown in the following examples (Figure 5), after Polybius.

2-5 Entrance to Roman Field Forts

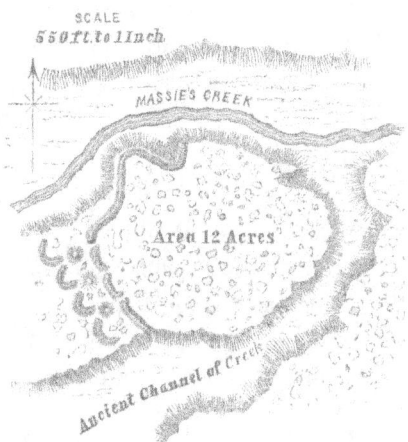

2-6 Massey's Creek Fort, Green County Ohio

Examples of "Hill Forts," similar to those here given, and each perhaps possessing some peculiar and interesting feature, might be greatly multiplied. Our purpose, however, is only to illustrate the general character of the ancient works, and not to exhaust the subject, which would require volumes to its complete elucidation. We turn, then, to another class of defensive structures, already alluded to as "occupying peninsulas or bluff points of land," naturally protected on most sides by streams or bold and inaccessible banks, or deep ravines. Of this variety of works Figure 6 is a good example. It is situated on Massey's Creek, a tributary of the Little

47

Miami River, seven miles east of Xenia, Green County, Ohio, occupying a high promontory bounded on all sides, except an interval on the west, by precipitous limestone cliffs. Across the neck of land where the cliff is interrupted is carried a wall of earth and stones, from which the ground subsides toward the adjacent plain with almost the regularity of an artificial glacis. This wall is now about ten feet high by thirty feet base, and is continued for some distance along the edge of the cliff, where it is least precipitous, on the north. It is interrupted by three narrow gateways, exterior to each of which there was formerly a mound of stones; now, however, in great part removed. Still exterior to these are four short crescent walls, together extending quite across the isthmus, constituting an outer line of defense. These crescents are rather slight, now not much exceeding three feet in height. The cliff, which protects the position on the remaining sides, has an average height of twenty-five feet, and is steep and almost inaccessible. At (d d) there are breaks in the limestone, where the declivity is sufficiently gentle to admit of ascent on horseback; and at (e) is a fissure, through which a man may ascend on foot. The valley, or rather ravine, (C C), is three hundred feet broad. Massey's Creek, a considerable stream, washes the base of the promontory on the north. The area, bounded by the cliff and wall, is not far from twelve acres, and is covered with the primitive forest. The natural strength of the position is obviously great; and if a line of palisades were carried along the brow of the cliff and summit of the wall the work would be almost impregnable to savage assault.

A simpler form of this class of works is afforded in Figure 7, which occurs in Oxford township, Butler County, Ohio, at a point on Four Mile Creek, where that stream takes a remarkable bend, forming a peninsula 1060 feet across its neck, and 1320 feet deep. This peninsula is elevated sixty feet above the waters of the creek, with precipitous banks, and overlooks the low "bottoms" which surround it. Across the neck of this peninsula is carried a crescent shaped wall, with an outer ditch; the former is now only about three feet high, and the latter of corresponding depth. Formerly the wall was much higher, precluding cultivation; but the present occupant of the land has plowed along it longitudinally, throwing the furrows into the ditch, and will soon obliterate it entirely. A single gateway, twenty feet wide, leads into the inclosure, which has an area of about

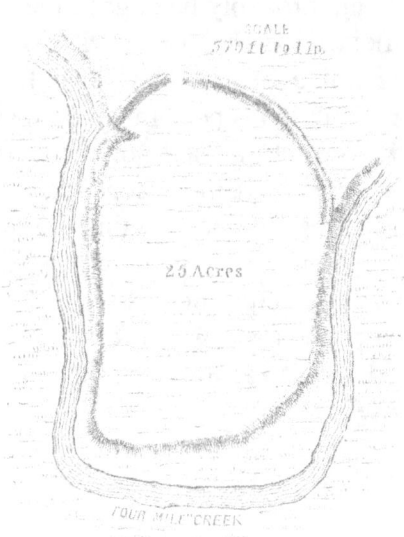

2-7 Defensive Work, Butler County Ohio

twenty-five acres. The creek, at one time, unquestionably ran close under the banks of the peninsula; but whether or not the recession of the stream, leaving the intervening low "bottom," took place subsequently to the erection of the work, it is now impossible to determine. In this work will be remarked a lapping round of the wall, on the natural bank of the stream at (b), a feature heretofore mentioned as probably designed to protect the flank of the defense.

Another example of this class of defensive structures will sufficiently illustrate their character. Figure 8 is a plan of a work, with a double line of walls, found on the Great Miami River, four miles southwest of the town of Hamilton, Butler County, Ohio. The outer line of defense consists of a simple embankment five feet high, with an exterior ditch four feet deep. It has a single gateway fifteen feet wide. There are two apparent entrances where the ditch only is interrupted. Interior to this line of embankment is another, of less dimensions, having also but one opening. At (a m) is a broad mound, over which, and somewhat below its summit, on its outer side, the second line of embankment is carried. The ditch is also continued uninterruptedly over the mound, which is thirty feet high. From its summit a view of the entire work and of the surrounding country is commanded. Another mound, ten feet high, occurs at the point indicated in the plan. It is composed of stone and gravel, apparently taken from the river, and probably belongs to the class of mounds denominated "sacrificial," the characteristics of which will appear further on. The outer wall appears to have been formerly extended down to a lower level; but it has been much obliterated by the washing of the bank. The natural banks on the west toward the river and next to Big Run are inaccessibly steep, and between sixty and seventy feet high. The area embraced within the exterior line of wall is a trifle less than eighteen acres. The defensive purposes of the work will hardly be called in question. It seems probable that the high mound over which the inner wall is carried was designed as a lookout or alarm post, as well as a kind of citadel, commanding the second line of defense.

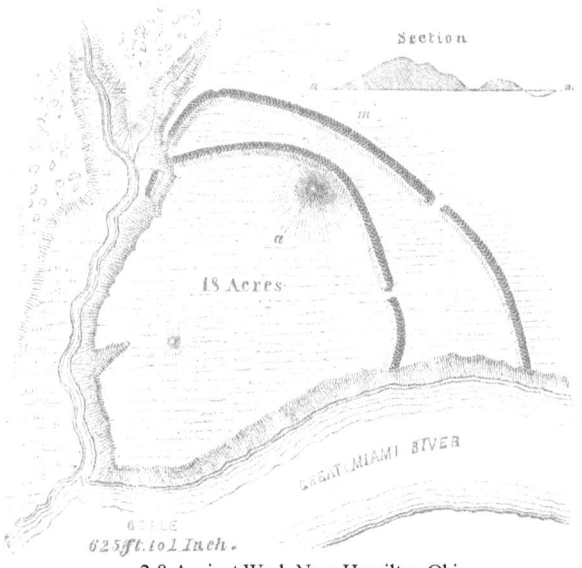

2-8 Ancient Work Near Hamilton Ohio

There remains to be considered another variety of works in which defensive features predominate, but which seem rather to have been fortified towns or villages than strongholds or citadels for final resort in case of danger. The natural conditions favorable for structures of the latter description, high hills, difficult of access, away from grounds most fertile and easy of cultivation, etc., etc., are not those most favorable for permanent residence in time of peace. It is not impossible, therefore, that in places admitting of it, the villages of

50

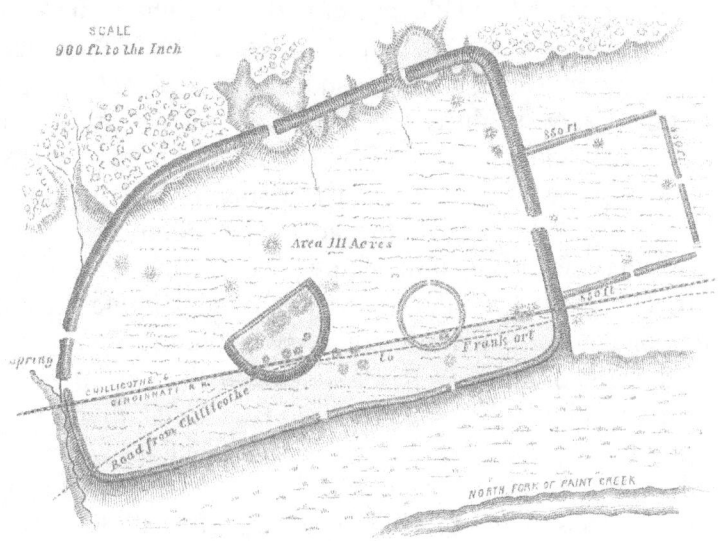

SCALE
900 ft. to the Inch

Area III Acres

spring

Road from Chillicothe

NORTH FORK OF PAINT CREEK

2-9 Ancient Works on North Fork of Paint Creek, Ohio

the mound builders were occasionally fortified, if not in a way to afford most effectual resistance, at least sufficiently to guard against surprise or sudden assault. Such, at any rate, appears to have been the case with the large and interesting work of which Figure 9 is a plan. It is situated on the North Fork of Paint Creek, in Ross County, Ohio, about five miles northwest of the city of Chilicothe, occupying the entire width of the second terrace of the valley, which is here a broad and level plain of exceeding beauty and fertility. Its general form is that of a parallelogram, 2800 feet long, by 1800 feet broad. On the side next the creek it is bounded by a wall of earth four feet high, running along the very edge of the terrace bank, which is about thirty feet in height, and conforming to its irregularities. Its remaining sides are defined by a wall and exterior ditch, the former six feet high by thirty feet base, and the latter of corresponding dimensions. The lines ascend the acclivity of the table land back of the terrace, and extend along its brow, dipping into the little ravines and rising over the ridges into which it has been cut by the action of water. Wherever these ravines are of any considerable depth the wall has been washed away—in all cases, however, leaving traces which favor the belief that it once extended uninterruptedly through them. The table land referred to has a general elevation of about fifty feet

51

above the terrace on which the work is principally situated. The area inclosed is one hundred and eleven acres. To the right of the principal work, and connecting with it by a gateway, is a smaller work of sixteen acres area, a perfect square, its sides measuring each 850 feet. It has gateways thirty feet wide at the middle of each side, covered by small mounds, placed fifty feet interior to the walls. There are also gateways at its two exterior corners; but these are not covered by mounds like those at the sides. The opening or gateway between this and the principal inclosure is double the width of the others. The walls of the smaller inclosure are much lighter than those of the large one, and are unaccompanied by a ditch.

Within the area of the great work are two small inclosures; one of them is a perfect circle, three hundred and fifty feet in diameter, consisting of a single light embankment, with a gateway opening to the west; the other is a semicircular inclosure, two thousand feet in circumference, consisting of a slight wall and ditch, as shown in the plan. Embraced in this last named inclosure are seven mounds, three of which are of large size and joined together, forming a continuous elevation thirty feet high, five hundred feet long, and one hundred and eighty feet broad at the base. These are shown in the plan. The ground within this subordinate inclosure appears to be elevated above the general level of the plain, probably from the wasting away of the inclosed mounds. There are other mounds both in this and the ground inclosure, at the points indicated in the plan, most of which have been explored, with very interesting results. Nearly all of these were found to belong to the class denominated altar or sacrificial mounds.

Where the walls of the great inclosure descend from the table land to the left is a gully or bed of a small stream, which, before the construction of this work, kept the course indicated by the dotted line, but was turned by the builders from its natural channel into the ditch, through which it still flows for a considerable distance. In one place it has broken over the wall, obliterating it for a distance of nearly two hundred feet. It is dry at most seasons of the year, and, unless much swollen, keeps within the ditch, which terminates in a deep ravine formed by the flow of water from a copious and unfailing spring, toward which opens a gateway. This artificial change in water courses has been observed in other works in various parts of the country.

The gateways of the main work are six in number, one opening into the smaller square inclosure, two leading out on the table land, one to the spring just mentioned, and others toward the creek to the southward. Two considerable springs occur within the work; but it is not necessary, on the hypothesis advanced as to its purposes, to suppose that its ancient occupants were wholly dependent on these sources for their supply of water, since it is very evident that many centuries may not have elapsed since the creek, now a hundred rods distant, washed the base of the terrace on which it stands on the south.

The slight wall along the terrace bank is chiefly composed of smooth, water worn stones taken from the creek and cemented together by a tough, clayey earth. The wall of the square is wholly of clay, which contrasts strongly, when plowed, with the dark loam of the terrace. In common with the embankments of many similar works it appears to have been slightly burned. This appearance is so marked as to induce the belief, in some minds, that the walls were originally composed of half burned bricks, which, in the lapse of time, have lost their form and subsided in a homogeneous mass. That in some instances they have been subjected to the action of fire is too obvious to admit of doubt. At the point in this work indicated by the letter (z), stones and large masses of pebbles and earth, much burned, and resembling a ferruginous conglomerate, are frequently turned up by the plow. This feature may perhaps be accounted for by supposing the walls to have been originally surmounted by palisades, or wooden structures of some kind, which were destroyed by fire.

As bearing upon the probable character of the work, it should be observed that the points of the table land on which the gateways at (I) and (S) open are natural bastions, in great part detached from the general level of the table.

Such are some of the features of this most interesting work, and if their detail has been somewhat tedious, it must be remembered that minute circumstances are often of first importance in getting at correct conclusions. The comparative slightness of the walls, and the absence of a ditch at the points naturally protected, the extension of the artificial defenses on the table land, overlooking and commanding the terrace, the abundant supply of water, as well as the large area inclosed, with its mysterious circles and sacred mounds, all go very far to show that this was a fortified town of the ancient people—a conclusion further sustained by the abundant fragments of pottery, large quantities of calcined bones, burned stones, ashes, and other evidences of occupancy scattered all over its area. The amount of labor which was expended on this work, in view of the probably limited means at the command of the builders, must have been very great. The embankments taken together measure nearly three miles in length, and a careful computation shows that not less than 3,000,060 cubic feet of earth were used in their construction and that of the inclosed *tumuli*. In this work have been made some of the most interesting discoveries in the way of ancient art with which we are acquainted, to which further reference will be made when we come to treat of that branch of our subject.

These examples are sufficiently numerous to convey a very clear notion of the ancient works classified as defensive; and no one can rise from an examination of them without being impressed with the degree of judgment and skill which they exhibit, and which seems very clearly to have surpassed that common to most of the North American Indian tribes at the period of the Discovery. Their magnitude must also impress the inquirer with enlarged notions of the power of the people commanding the means for their construction, and whose numbers required such extensive works for their protection. It is not impossible that they were, to a certain extent, designed to embrace cultivated fields, so as to furnish the means of sustenance to their defenders in event of a protracted siege. There is no other foundation, however, for this suggestion than is furnished by the size of some of these defensive inclosures. The population finding shelter within their walls must have been exceedingly large, if their dimensions may be taken as the basis of a calculation.

The vast amount of labor necessary to the erection of most of these works precludes the notion that they were hastily constructed to check a single or unexpected invasion. On the contrary, there seems to have existed a System of Defenses extending from the sources of the Allegheny, in New York, diagonally across the country, through central Ohio to the Wabash. Within this range those works which are regarded as defensive are largest and most numerous. If an inference may be drawn from this fact, it is that the pressure of hostilities was from the northeast; or that, if the tide of migration was from the south, it was arrested on this line. On the

54

other hand, on the hypothesis that in this region originated a semi-civilization which subsequently spread southward, constantly developing itself in its progress until it attained its height in Mexico, we may suppose from this direction came the hostile savage hordes, before whose incessant attacks the less warlike mound builders gradually receded, or beneath whose exterminating cruelty they entirely disappeared —leaving these monuments alone to attest their existence, and the extraordinary skill with which they defended their altars and their homes. Upon either assumption it is clear that the contest was a protracted one, and that the race of the mounds were for a long period constantly exposed to attack. This conclusion finds its support in the fact that, in the vicinity of those localities, where, from the amount of remains, it appears the ancient population was most dense, we almost invariably find one or more works of a defensive character, furnishing ready places of resort in times of danger. We may suppose that a state of things existed somewhat analogous to that which attended the advance of our pioneer population, when every settlement had its little fort, to which the settlers flocked in case of alarm or attack.

It may be suggested that there existed among the mound builders a state of society something like that which prevailed among the Indians; that each tribe had its separate seat, maintaining an almost constant warfare against its neighbors, and, as a consequence, possessing its own "castle," as a place of final resort when invaded by a powerful foe. Apart from the fact, however, that the Indians were hunters, averse to labor, and not known to have constructed any works approaching, in skillfulness of design or in magnitude, those under notice, there is almost positive evidence that the mound builders were an agricultural people, considerably advanced in the arts, and possessing great uniformity, throughout the whole territory which they occupied, in manners, habits, and religion—a uniformity sufficiently marked to identify them as a single people, having a common origin, common modes of life, and, as a consequence, common sympathies, if not a common and consolidated government.

## Sacred Inclosures

[Frequently of immense size; situated generally on level ground; regular in outline usually circular, square, or octagonal, or with all these figures combined; sometimes with a long cursus, or ranges of parallel walls, combined with or dependent on them; generally with no ditch, but if a ditch, interior to the walls; entrances at regular intervals, in the circles commonly opening to the east; often with a mound in the geometrical center, and others in a certain fixed relation to the principal features of the work.]

There is another and more numerous class of inclosures in the West, which it is evident, from their structure, not less than from their form and position, were not designed for defense. For reasons which will appear more clearly as we proceed, they have been classified as Sacred Inclosures, in some way connected with the religious notions, rites, and ceremonies of their builders. They are generally exceedingly regular in their design, frequently geometrically so, and occupy the broad and level river bottoms, seldom occurring on the table lands, or where the surface of the ground is undulating or broken. Their usual form is that of the square or the circle—circular works being, however, most numerous. Occasionally we find them isolated, but oftenest in groups. The greater number of the circles are of small size, having a nearly uniform diameter of two hundred and fifty or three hundred feet. These have always a single gateway, opening oftenest toward the east, but by no means observing a fixed rule in this respect. It frequently happens that they have one or more small mounds interior to their walls, of the class denominated sacrificial. These small circles occasionally occur within larger works of a defensive character. Apart from these, numerous smaller circles, from thirty to fifty feet in diameter, are observed in the vicinity of large works, consisting of a very light embankment of earth, and destitute of a gateway or entrance. It has been suggested that these are the remains of the ancient lodges or of other buildings. It sometimes happens that we find small circles around the bases of large mounds; but these probably can not be regarded as of the same character with that numerous class already referred to.

A characteristic feature of all these works, and that which distinguishes them from works of defense, is the almost invariable absence of a ditch, or its occurrence within instead of exterior to the walls. Another circumstance favoring the same conclusion, apart from the small size of many of them, is that they are often completely commanded from adjacent heights. We must therefore seek, in the connection in which these works are found, and in the character and contents of the mounds, if such there be, within their walls for the secret of their design. And it may be observed that it is here that we discover evidence still more satisfactory and conclusive than is furnished by the small dimensions of these works, or the position of the ditch, that they were not intended for defense. Thus, when we find inclosures containing a number of mounds, all of which, it is capable of demonstration, were religious in their purposes, or in some way connected with the superstitions of the people who built them, the conclusion is irresistible that the inclosure was esteemed sacred, and thus set apart as consecrated ground.

But it is not to be concluded that those inclosures which contain mounds of this description were alone designed for sacred purposes. We have reason to believe that the religious system of the mound builders, like that of the Mexicans, exercised among them a great, if not a controlling influence. Their government may have been, for aught we know, a government of the priesthood; one in which the priestly and civil functions were jointly exercised, and one sufficiently powerful to have secured in the Mississippi Valley, as it did in Mexico and Central America, the erection of many of those vast monuments, which for ages will continue to challenge the wonder of men. There may have been certain superstitious ceremonies, having no connection with the purposes of the mounds, carried on in inclosures specially dedicated to them. There are several minor inclosures within the great defensive work, already referred to, on the banks of the North Fork of Paint Creek (Figure 9), the purposes of which would scarcely admit of doubt, even though the sacred mounds which they embrace were wanting. It is a conclusion which every day's investigation and observation has tended to confirm, that most, perhaps all the earth works, not manifestly defensive in their character, were in some way connected with the superstitious rites of the builders, though in what manner, it is, and perhaps ever will be, impossible satisfactorily to determine.

What dim light analogy sheds upon this point goes to sustain this conclusion. The "ring forts" of the ancient Celts are nearly identical in form and structure with a large class of remains in our own country; and these are regarded by all well informed British antiquaries as strictly religious in their origin, or connected with the rites of the ancient Druidical system. This conclusion is not entirely speculative, but rests in a great degree upon traditional and historical facts. Borlase observes, "The grandeur of design, the distance of the materials, the tediousness with which all such massive works are erected, all show that they were the fruits of peace and religion." "That they were erected," says Hoare, "for the double purpose of civil and religious assemblies, may be admitted without controversy. They were public edifices, constructed according to the rude fashion of the times, and at a period when the Deity was worshiped in the most simple and primitive manner, under the open canopy of heaven."

Caesar, writing of the Druids, is understood to allude to their sacred structures in the following terms: "Once a year the Druids assemble at a consecrated place. Hither such as have suits depending flock from all parts, and submit implicitly to their decrees." It need not be added that the Druids were priests and judges, the expounders of religion and the administrators of justice; they were intrusted with the education of youth, and taught the motions of the stars, the magnitude of the earth, the nature of things, and the dignity and power of the gods. They officiated at sacrifices and divinations; they decided controversies, punished the guilty, and rewarded the virtuous. Their power was superior to that of the nobles,over whom they wielded the terrors of excommunication from a participation in the imperative rites of their religion. they centered in themselves the occult learning of the day, which seems to have been closely allied to that of Phoenicia, if not, indeed, mainly derived from the East.

The small circles to which we have alluded, as well as others of large size, are often found in combination with rectangular works, connecting with them directly or by avenues. In some instances these circles embrace fifty or more acres, and, as in the case of the squares or rectangular works with which they are attached (and which, it is believed, never have ditches, exterior or interior), the walls are usually composed of earth taken up evenly from the surface, or from large pits in the neighborhood. Evident care seems, in all cases, to have been exercised in procuring the material, to preserve the surface of the adjacent plain smooth, and as far as possible unbroken. The walls of these works are, for the most part, comparatively slight, varying from three to seven feet in height. Sometimes they are quite imposing, as in the case of the great circle at Newark, Licking County, Ohio, where, at the entrance, the wall from the bottom of the ditch has a vertical height of not far from thirty feet. The square or rectangular works attending these large circles are of various dimensions. It has been observed, however, that certain groups are marked by a great uniformity of size. Five or six of these now occur to the writer, placed at long distances asunder, which are exact squares, each measuring one thousand and eighty feet side—a coincidence which could not possibly be accidental, and which must possess some significance. It certainly establishes the existence of some standard of measurement among the ancient people, if not the possession of some means of determining angles. The rectangular works have almost invariably gateways at the angles and midway on each side, each of which is coveted by a small interior mound or elevation. In some of the larger structures the openings are more numerous. A few of this description of remains have been discovered which are octagonal. One of large size, in the vicinity of Chilicothe, has the alternate angles coincident with each other, and the sides equal.

Another description of works, probably akin to those here described, are the parallels, consisting of light embankments, seven or eight hundred feet in length, and sixty or eighty apart.

Indeed so various are these works, and so numerous their combinations, that it is impossible to convey any accurate conception of them without entering into a minuteness of detail and an extent of illustration utterly beyond the limits of this paper. If we are right in the assumption that they are of sacred origin, and were the temples and consecrated grounds of the ancient people, we can, from their number and extent, form some estimate of the devotional fervor or superstitious zeal which induced their erection, and the predominance of the religious sentiment among their builders.

Figure 10 affords a good illustration of the simpler forms of the structures under notice. The group occurs on the banks of Paint Creek, about two miles to the southwest of the city of Chilicothe, Ohio, and consists of four circles, three crescents, two square works, and four mounds. The inclosure (A) is the largest, and, in common

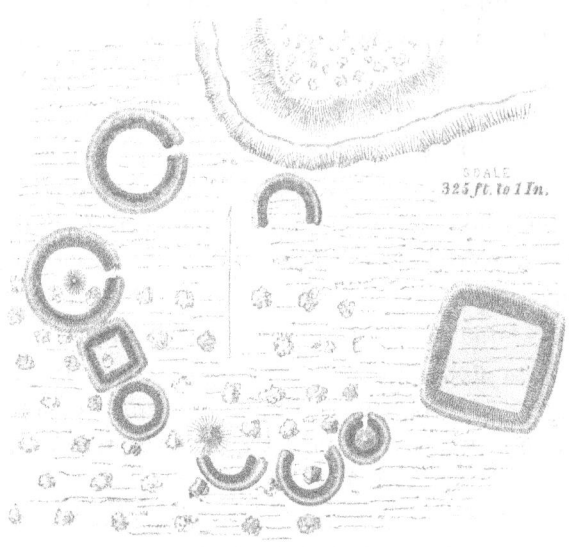

2-10 Group of Works on Paint Creek Ohio

with all the rest, consists of a wall three feet high, with an interior ditch. The walls at its sides are each two hundred and forty feet long, much curved, so as to give it exteriorly somewhat the form of a circle. The area bounded by the ditch is, however, an exact square of one hundred and sixty feet side, entered from the south by a gateway twenty-five feet broad. A little to the south and left of this inclosure is a mound, (B), three feet high, surrounded by a ditch and exterior embankment, the ditch and wall being interrupted for a narrow space on the north, so form a gateway or level approach to the mound. The peculiarities of the other works of the group are sufficiently obvious from the plan. The mound (E), in which one of the crescent shaped works terminates, is seven feet high by forty-five feet base, and was excavated in 1845. It was found to belong to the class denominated sacred. That these works were not defensive is obvious; and that they were dedicated to religious purposes seems more than probable.

A group somewhat analogous to that last described occurs on the east bank of the Scioto River, eight miles north of Chilicothe (Figure 11). It is, however, distinguished by two singular parallels, (A) and (B) of the plan, each of which is seven hundred and fifty feet long by sixty broad, measuring from center to center of the parallel embankments. They are in cultivated grounds, and the walls are

60

much reduced, being scarcely two feet high. A gateway opens into the southern parallel from the east, and a corresponding opening may have existed in the other; but, if so, it is no longer traceable.

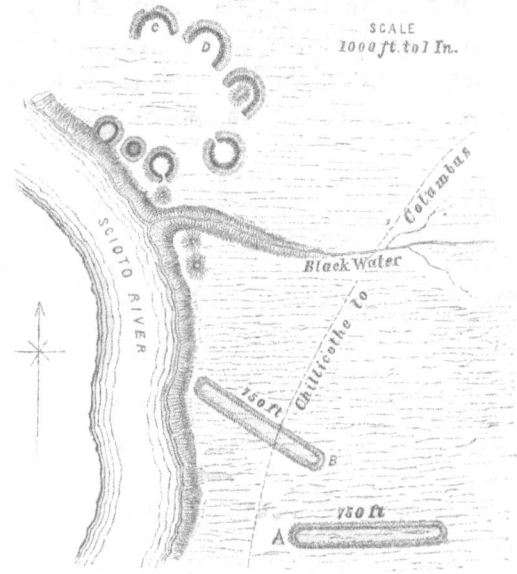

2-11 Circles and Parallells

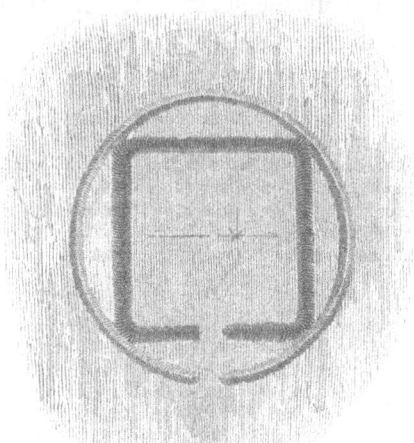

2-12 Ancient Work, Pike County Ohio

In some cases a square is defined by means of a ditch inside of a circle, as shown in Figure 12, which occurs in connection with a large and singular group of ancient works in Pike County, Ohio. The circle consists of an embankment five feet high, and is three hundred feet in diameter; the ditch is three feet deep, and the square which it forms is two hundred feet on each side.

A little more than a mile to the northward of the work last described is another quite unique, of which Figure 13 is a plan. Its walls are about four feet high, and its outlines beautifully distinct, having as yet escaped the encroachments of the plow.

2-13 Ancient Work, Pike County Ohio

Figure 14 is an example of an isolated circle, of large size, on the right bank of the Great Miami River, seven miles below the town of Hamilton. The embankment is about two feet high, composed of earth taken up evenly from the surface, terminating on either hand in small mounds, between four and five feet high. The inclosed area is level, and covered with forest. The area is about twenty-six acres.

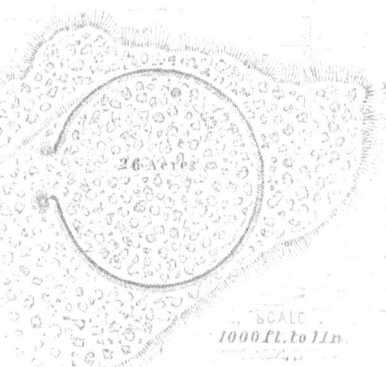

2-14 Circular Work on Great Miami River

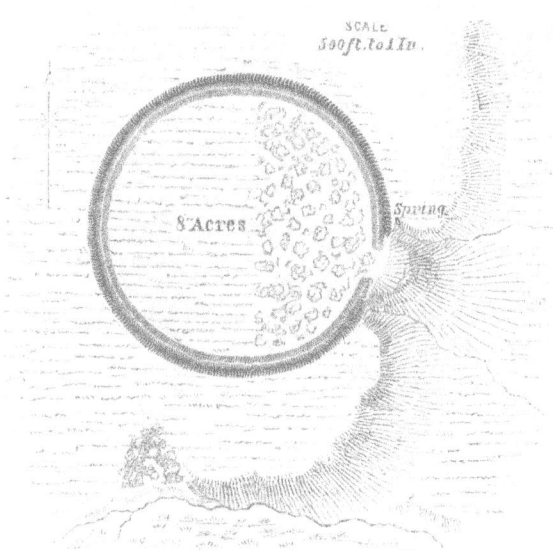

2-15 Elliptical Work Near Bourneville Ohio

Figure 15 is a plan of an elliptical work, one of the best preserved and most beautiful in the State of Ohio. It is situated on the highest river terrace, directly facing, and about one mile distant from the great defensive structure already described (Figure 2). It consists of a wall of earth between eight and ten feet in height, with a broad and shallow exterior ditch. As already stated, it is elliptical, having a transverse diameter of seven hundred and fifty feet, and a conjugate diameter of six hundred and seventy-five feet. It has but a single gateway, one hundred and twenty feet wide, opening to the southwest, on a small spur of the terrace which seems to have been artificially rounded and graded, so as to make a regular and easy descent to the lower level. On both sides of this graded declivity the banks are steep and irregular. A small circle and a couple of mounds are situated in the next lower terrace, at the points indicated in the plan. This work is remarkable as being the only one known of a circular form with its ditch exterior to its wall. As already stated, this ditch is broad and shallow, and does not show design; in other words, instead of bringing the earth for the embankment from holes and at a distance, or collecting it evenly from the adjacent plain, the builders — from haste, or other cause—gathered it on the spot, the ditch being only the accidental result of their excavations.

63

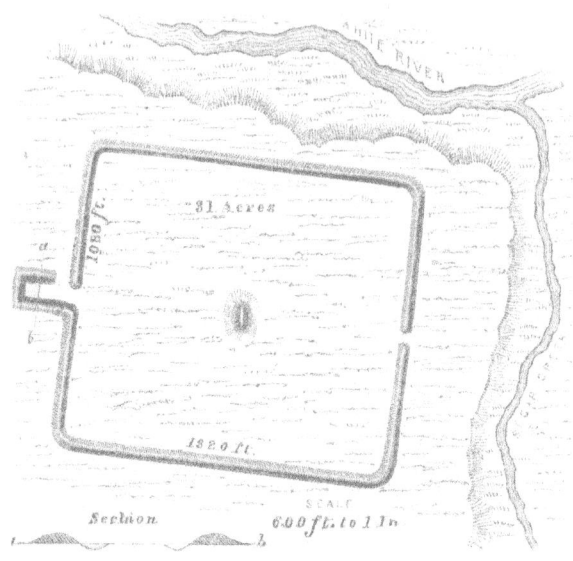

2-16 Rectangular Work Randolph County Indiana

While detached circles of various sizes are frequent, there are very few detached square or rectangular works. As elsewhere stated, these almost invariably occur in combination with circles. Figure 16 is, nevertheless, an example of a great rectangle of remarkable beauty and regularity, near the town of Winchester, Randolph County, Indiana. Its character is sufficiently indicated from the plan. The walls, it will be observed, are unaccompanied by a ditch, excepting the lighter wall covering the entrance from the left, which has a ditch on its inner side. A work precisely similar to this, but of smaller size, occurs a few miles distant, on the upper waters of Sugar Creek. Between the two is a copious spring, surrounded by a ring or circle of earth—suggesting an analogy with the sacred and protected springs and trees of the ancient Celts and the Sandwich Islanders.

Another rectangular work—which, however, has some characteristics of a defensive structure—is found five miles to the north of the city of Chilicothe, on the left bank of the Scioto River. Figure 17 is a plan. It has a wall and outer ditch, forming three sides of a parallelogram; the fourth side being protected by a natural bank seventy feet high, close at the foot of which flows the river. The walls are six feet high by forty feet base, and the ditch five feet deep and forty feet wide. This ditch, on the eastern side, is formed by a

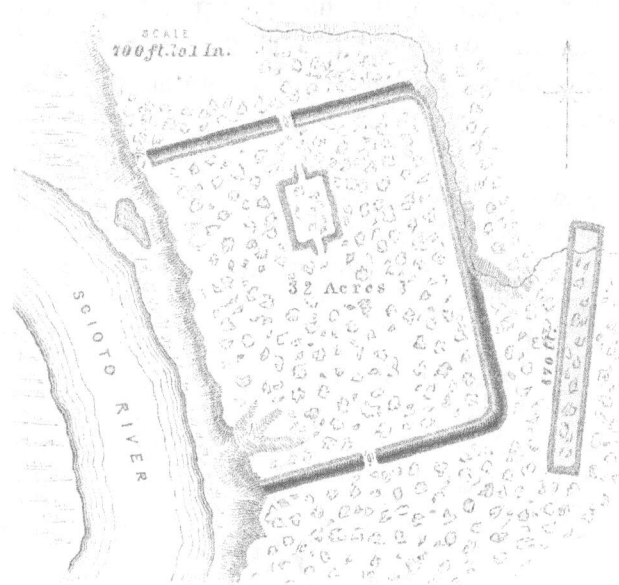

2-17 Cedar Bank Works Ohio

waterway or gullet, between eight and ten feet deep—in part, perhaps, artificial. There are gateways, each sixty feet wide, at the centers of the northern and southern sides. Two hundred feet interior to that on the north, and covering it, is a square mound, two hundred and forty-five feet long and one hundred and fifty broad; four feet high, with graded ascents at the ends, thirty feet wide. To the right of the main work, and about three hundred feet distant from it, are singular parallel walls, resembling those previously described (Figure 11), eight hundred and seventy feet long and seventy feet apart, joined at the ends. These walls lave no ditch, and have been partially obliterated by the Chilicothe and Columbus turnpike, which runs through them. About a third of a mile to the southward of the principal work are the singular circle and truncated pyramid represented in Figure 18.

The latter is one hundred and twenty feet square at the base, and nine feet in height; the former is two hundred and fifty feet in diameter, and has an entrance on the south thirty feet wide. It has a ditch interior to the embankment, and also a broad embankment, of about the same elevation with the outer wall, interior to the ditch, on the side opposite to the entrance. This feature, which is observable in

65

many of the smaller circles, is well exhibited in the plan and section. Two sides of the pyramidal structure correspond with the cardinal points. It has been excavated, but no remains were found in it. It is difficult to determine the character of this group of works. The principal work partakes of the nature of a defense; but the broad gateways, the rectangular elevation within the walls, and the adjacent parallels, are hardly consistent with the hypothesis of a military origin, and seem rather to connect it with the class of works devoted to religious purposes, games, or other observances, of which we can only conjecture the nature.

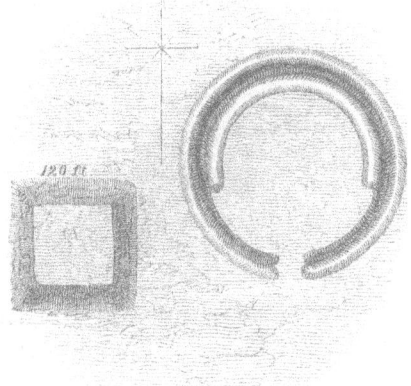

2-18 Works Near Cedar Bank

The comparatively small work which is represented in Figure 19 is found in Fairfield County, Ohio, seven miles from the town of Lancaster, on the road to Columbus, near a place known as "Hocking River Upper Falls." It is remarkable as being situated on the level summit of a hill, two hundred feet above the river. Advantage is taken of the slightly undulating character of the ground, so that the small circle inclosing the mound overlooks every part of the work, and commands a wide prospect on every hand. Two elliptical terraces, a few feet in height, occur outside of the work, near the brow of the hill. They are not included in the plan.

We come now to a class of regular works of larger size, combining the square and circle. The first example (Figure 20) is a work occurring four miles north of the city of Chilicothe, on the left bank of the Scioto River. It consists of a rectangle and attached

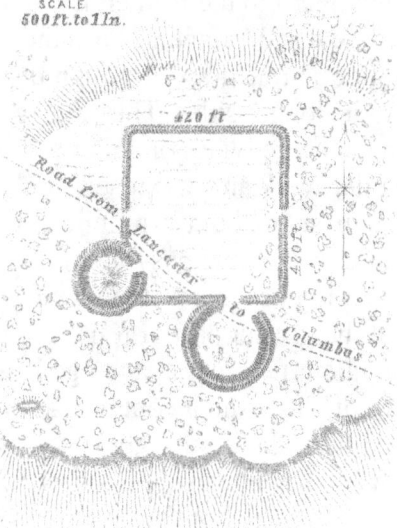

2-19 Square Work, Fairfield County Ohio

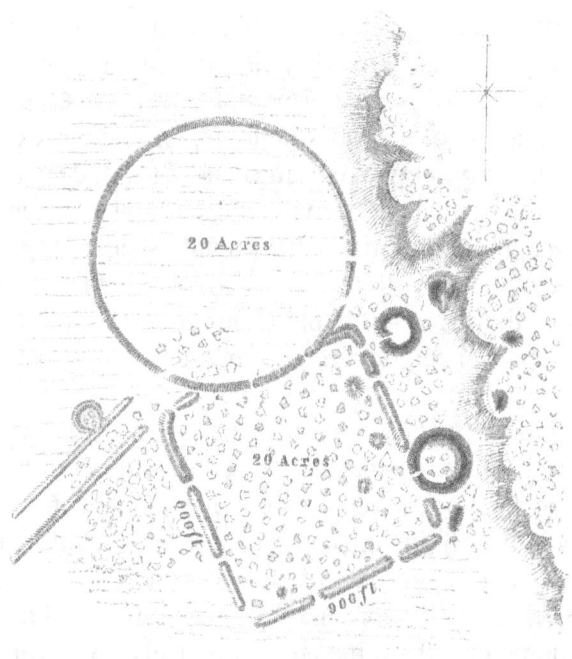

circle, the latter extending into the former, instead of being connected with it in the usual manner. The center of the circle is somewhat to the right of a line drawn through the center of the rectangle, parallel to its longer sides. The gateways are twelve in number, and have an average width of about twenty-five feet. The walls of the rectangular work are composed of a clayey loam, twelve feet high by fifty feet base, without exterior or interior ditch, and broad enough on top to permit the passage of a coach. The wall of the circle was never as high as that of the rectangle; but notwithstanding that the greater part of it has long been under cultivation, it is still about five feet in average height. It is without ditch, and composed of clay, which contrasts strongly with the dark color of the surrounding soil. To the right of the rectangle, and between it and the bank of the next superior terrace, are two small circles, the walls of which are about three feet high, with interior ditches. About two hundred paces to the north of the great circle is also another small one, two hundred and fifty-five feet in diameter. Leading of from the work, to the southwest, are parallel walls, a small portion of which are represented in the plan. They are one hundred and fifty feet apart, nearly half a mile long, reaching to the edge of the terrace on which the principal works are situated. Near the southeastern angle of the work, and also on the bank of the superior terrace, are great pits, or "dug holes" (d, d, d), from whence large quantities of earth have been taken, though much less, apparently, than enters into the embankments. There are no mounds of magnitude connected with this work—none, in fact, except the small elevations indicated in the plan. On the opposite bank of the Scioto River, however, in the direction pursued by the parallels, there are several large groups.

Five miles below the city of Chilicothe, on the right bank of the Scioto River, is found the beautiful work represented in the plan (Figure 21). It occurs at a place where the river has cut its way up to the third terrace, which, in consequence, presents a bold bank between seventy and eighty feet high. The principal work consists of a combined circle and octagon, the former 950 feet and the latter 1050 feet in diameter—the dimensions precisely coinciding, it will be observed, with those of the work last described (Figure 20). The octagon is not strictly regular, although its alternate angles are coincident and its sides equal. The circle is perfect in form, as are also the smaller and dependent circles observable in the plan. Near the lower left hand angle of the octagon are two circles—one quite small, the other 300 feet in diameter—from which lead off two converging lines of embankment, connecting with a series of circles of varying sizes, half a mile distant to the southwest. Still beyond these, on the bank of the terrace, is a large truncated mound, 30 feet in height. A number of small circles, each about 50 feet in diameter, with walls two feet in height, occur a hundred rods to the southward of the principal work, in the midst of a forest.

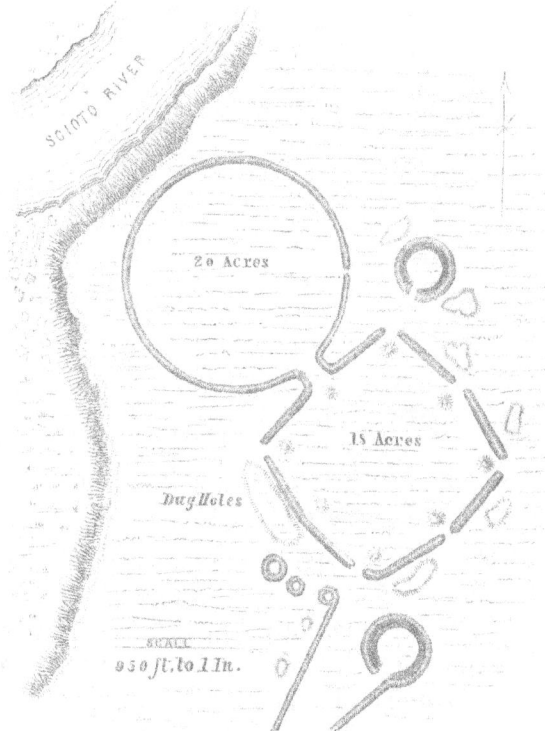

2-21 High Bank Works Ohio

Of the class of regular or sacred works under notice Figure 22 is nearly a perfect example. It is situated on the third river terrace, on the east bank of the Scioto River, eight miles to the southeast of the city of Chilicothe, on the road to Richmondale and Jackson. The terrace is here beautifully level and unbroken. It will be observed that the work consists of three circles and a square, the latter

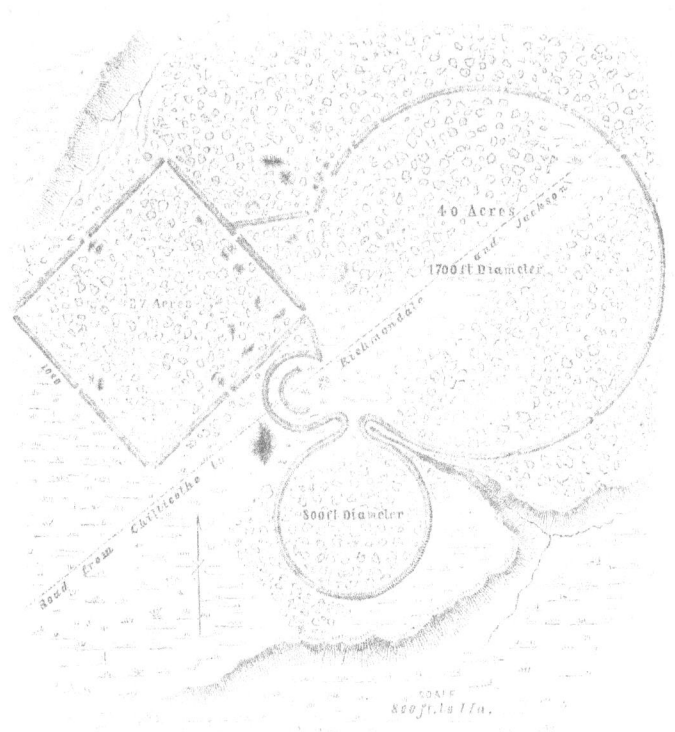

2-22 Ancient Work, Liberty Township, Ross County, Ohio

measuring 1080 feet on each side. Its walls are interrupted at each corner and at the middle of each side by gateways, each 30 feet wide. The central gateways are covered by low mounds, placed 40 feet interior to the line of the walls. The manner in which the circles are connected with each other and with the square is best shown by the plan, which precludes the necessity of a description. It will be observed that, while the embankment of the large circle is interrupted by numerous gateways, the walls of the smaller circles are entire throughout. Besides the small mounds at the gateways, there are three others within the work, the largest being 160 feet long by 20 feet high. It was excavated in 1846, and found to contain two sepulchral chambers. Numerous dug holes, or places whence earth had been taken for its construction, exist in its vicinity, as also in various other places within the square—a circumstance rather unusual. In fact, the whole work appears to have been but partially finished, or hastily built. The mounds near the gateways, and those

70

exterior to the walls, seem to have been formed by carelessly scooping up the earth at their bases, forming irregular pits of various depths. It is difficult to conceive the uses of a religious work of these vast dimensions; but it is still more difficult to believe that it has a military design. That there is some hidden significance, and probably some symbolical design, in the first place in the regularity, and secondly in the arrangement of the various parts of this work, can scarcely be doubted.

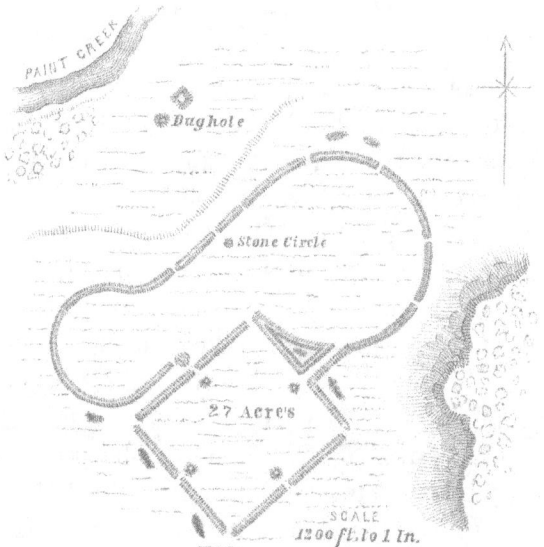

2-23 Ancient Work on Paint Creek

Figure 23 is only another illustration of the same class of works, of which that just described furnishes so complete an example. It differs from that in no essential respect, except that its walls are higher and heavier. It occurs on the right bank of Paint Creek, 14 miles above Chilicothe. The gateways are considerably wider than in most other works of this class, being not less than 70 feet across. A large, square, truncated mound occurs at some distance to the north of this work. It is 120 feet square at the base, 50 feet square at the top, and 15 feet high. Other works of precisely the same character and dimensions, but in which the square and circle are variously combined, are found in different parts of the Scioto Valley, of which numerous examples are given in the first volume of the "Smithsonian Contributions to Knowledge."

71

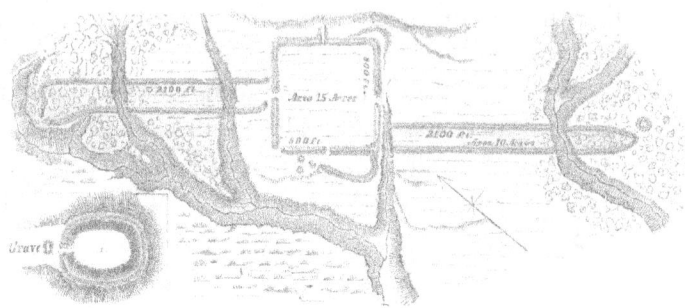

2-24 Ancient Work Near Portsmouth Ohio

Before dismissing this class of ancient works it will be indispensable to notice a subordinate variety of the class, less common, but not less interesting, of which Figure 24 is an example. It occurs on the Kentucky side of the Ohio River, near the mouth of the Scioto River, at Portsmouth. The river terrace on which it is situated is much cut up by ravines; but it is carried across them, notwithstanding, at right angles. The site of the square or main body of the work, nevertheless, is level and unbroken. It is an exact rectangle, 800 feet square, the walls about 12 feet high, by 35 or 40 feet base, except on the east, where advantage is taken of the rise of ground to elevate them about 50 feet above the center of the area. The hollow way between the southeastern wall and the terrace bank seems artificial, or, at any rate, adapted by art. On this side the gateway is entered by a slightly elevated causeway. At the southern angle is what appears to be a bastion, probably natural, but modified artificially, which commands the hollow way or ditch. On the southwestern side is a kind of runway, or ditch, which loses itself in a deep gully toward the river. There are no traces of ditches elsewhere about the work. A narrow gateway, 30 feet wide, opens in the middle of each side of the square, and at both the northern and western angles, as shown in the plan.

The most singular features of this work are its outworks, which consist of parallel walls leading off at right angles to the square, to the northeast and southwest, each 2100 feet long. The parallel to the southwest has its outer wall in line with the northwestern wall of the main work, and starts from it at a distance of 30 feet. It is broken by a deep ravine near its extremity, beyond which the walls curve inward on a radius of 100 feet, leaving only a space of eight feet between their extremities. Converging walls start from the point of curve, but lose themselves after running 300 feet, without meeting. Just beyond, on the plain, are two clay mounds, also a small circle 100 feet in diameter. The remaining parallel starts nearly from the center of the northeastern wall of the main work, and is in all respects similar to that just described, except in the mode of its termination, which can only be explained by the plan. The left wall of this parallel bends to a right angle as it approaches the main work.

At the point indicated by the letter (N), and 450 feet to the left of the second parallel, on a high peninsula or headland, is a singular redoubt, of which the supplementary figure, (B), is an enlarged plan. At its left is the bank of the second "bottom," or terrace, 50 feet high, and very steep. At its right is a ravine with steep banks. The embankment of this work is heavy, and the ditch, which is interior to the wall, is wide and deep. The inclosed oval is only 60 feet wide by 110 long. It has a gateway to the northeast 10 feet wide. The object of this inclosure is difficult to divine. Its position and the dimensions of its walls would seem to indicate a defensive purpose; but this hypothesis is combated by its small size.

The entire main work, the greater part of the lower parallel, and a portion of the upper one, are now in open, cultivated grounds. The walls of the square are too steep to admit of cultivation, and now form fence lines to the inclosure, which has an area of 15 acres. From the dimensions of the walls, and other circumstances, it has been supposed that this was a fortified place. But the parallel seem to be without a military design; and we are forced to consider it, from interior evidence, and from the relation which it sustains to a certain class of structures in the Old World, as of sacred origin.

Such is the character of a considerable portion of the ancient works of the Mississippi Valley. How far a faithful attention to their details has tended to sustain the position assigned to them at the outset the intelligent reader must determine. Their general great size is, perhaps, the strongest objection which can be urged against the hypothesis of a religious design. It is difficult to comprehend the existence of religious works extending, with their attendant avenues, like those near Newark in Ohio, over an area of little less than four square miles! We can find their parallels only in the great temples of Abury and Stonehenge in England, and Carnuc in Brittany, and associate them with a mysterious worship of the Sun, or an equally mysterious Sabianism. Within the mounds inclosed in many of these sacred works we find the altars upon which glowed their sacrificial fires, and where the ancient people offered their propitiations to the strange gods of their primitive superstition. These altars also furnish us with the too unequivocal evidence that the ritual of the mound builders, like that of the Aztecs, was disfigured by sanguinary observances, and that human sacrifices were not deemed unacceptable to the divinity of their worship. It is of course impossible in this connection to go into the details of the evidence upon this or kindred points of interest. These belong to works of a more purely scientific character.

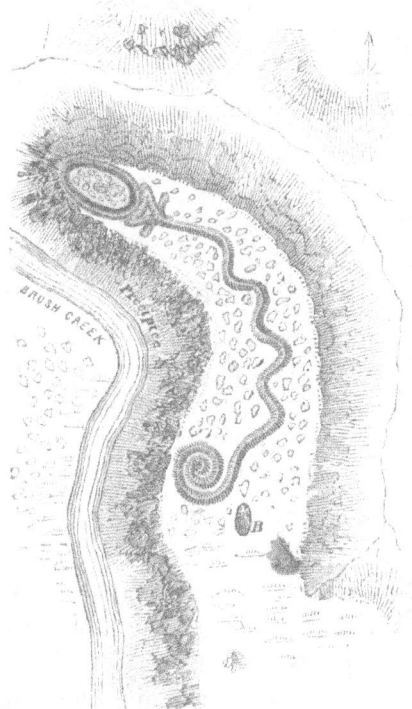

3-1 "Great Serpent" Adams County Ohio

DOUBTLESS of the same sacred and symbolical origin, but quite different from the works before described, is the singular serpentine structure represented in the accompanying plan (Figure 1). It is unquestionably, in many respects, the most extraordinary and interesting monument of antiquity yet discovered in the United States. It is situated on the right bank of Brush Creek, Adams County, Ohio, near a point known as "Three Forks," on the summit of a high crescent formed hill, elevated 150 feet above the level of the creek at its base. The hill presents toward the stream a perpendicular wall of rock, but on the opposite side slopes rapidly, but is not so abrupt as to preclude cultivation. The summit of the hill is not level, but slightly convex, presenting a surface about 150 feet wide and 1000 feet long, measuring from its extremity to the point where it connects with the table land, of which it may be regarded as a spur. Conforming to the longitudinal curve of the hill, and occupying its very summit, is an embankment artfully built in the form of a serpent, its head resting near the point of the hill, and its body winding back for 700 feet in graceful undulations, terminating in a triple coil at the tail. If extended, its entire length would be a little upward of 1000 feet. It is throughout clearly and boldly defined; the embankment being upward of five feet in height by thirty feet base at the middle of the body, but tapering in just proportion toward the head and tail. The neck is stretched out and slightly curved, and its mouth is opened wide, as if in the act of swallowing or ejecting an oval figure, which rests partially within its distended jaws. This oval is formed by an embankment of earth, without any perceptible opening, four feet in height, and perfectly regular in outline, its conjugate and transverse diameters being 160 and 80 feet respectively. The ground within this oval seems to be slightly raised above the general level; and a small circular elevation of large stones once existed in its center, but these have been thrown down and scattered by "money diggers." The point of the hill within which this oval figure rests seems to have been artificially cut and rounded to conform to the outline of the oval, leaving a smooth platform, ten feet wide and somewhat inclining inward, all around it. On each side of the serpents head are two small triangular elevations, ten or twelve feet broad. They are not high; and although too distinct to be overlooked, are yet too much obliterated to be satisfactorily traced. There is a "'platform" or low oval terrace at (B), and a large mound in the center of the isthmus connecting the hill or spur with the table land. An extensive prospect is commanded from all parts of the hill on which this effigy occurs; but no other works occur in its immediate vicinity.

Probably no one will hesitate in ascribing to this work some extraordinary significance. It can not be supposed to be the offspring of an idle fancy or a savage whim. In its position, and the harmony and elaboration of structure, it bears the evidences of design; and it seems to have been began and finished in accordance with a matured plan, and not to have been the result of successive and unmeaning combinations. It is palpably not a work of defense, for there is nothing to defend; on the contrary, it is clearly and unmistakably, in form and attitude, the representation of a serpent, with jaws distended, in the act of swallowing or ejecting an oval figure, which, from the suggestions of analogy, we shall distinguish as an egg. Assuming for the entire structure a religious origin, it can only be regarded as the recognized symbol of some grand mythological idea. What abstract conception was thus embodied, or what vast event thus typically commemorated, we have no certain means of knowing. Analogy, however, furnishes us with some gleams of light on the subject, which may assist us in arriving at an approximately correct conclusion concerning it. As in modern times Christian temples are generally constructed in the form of a cross, the symbol of the Christian faith, so in primitive times sacred structures were constructed in the form of predominant religious symbols. It is impossible to go into the rationale of this practice, which is equally natural and logical. The British islands afford us a number of illustrations, of which the great Serpentine temple of Abury, in Wiltshire, is among the best known. Although much dilapidated, it can still be distinctly traced. It consists of a circle 1400 feet in diameter, with an interior ditch. Extending from this, on either hand, were parallel lines of huge upright stones, constituting long avenues, each upward of a mile in length, so arranged as to represent the outline of a serpent, the head being indicated by an oval structure, made up of the concentric lines of upright stones, and resting on a hill which commanded a view of the entire structure. The details of the work, although interesting, are too numerous to be recounted here. It is, perhaps, enough to say, that however British antiquaries may differ in other respects, they all unite in recognizing in the work at Abury a representation of the serpent, and an exclusively sacred origin. Stukely supposes the entire structure to correspond to the sacred hierogram of the Egyptians, the circle or globe, the serpent, and outspread wings. A still more extensive work of the same symbolical import and design is that of Karnac, in Brittany, which has a length of several miles. At Stanton Drew, in England, is another of comparatively small size, represented in the following engraving (Figure 2) but of which the design is not so obvious. The central oval is 378 by 345 feet in diameter, and is connected, by curved parallels, with two smaller circles, as shown in the plan. All of these works have been shown to be connected in various ways with the worship of the Sun, of which the serpent was often, if not generally, regarded as a symbol. The evidence on this point is abundant and conclusive, but too voluminous to be embraced in an

77

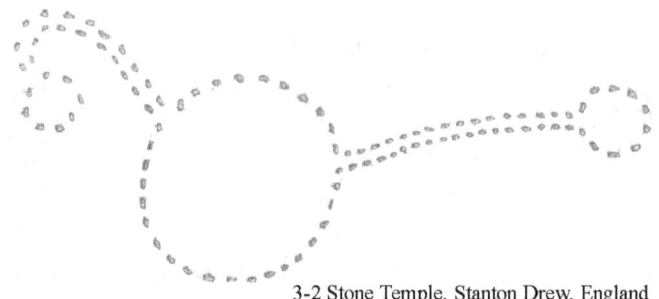

3-2 Stone Temple, Stanton Drew, England

article like this. This evidence goes to show also that the square was generally the symbol of the earth, and the circle of the sun, in that primitive system of religion and worship—a fact which throws some light on the class of works which we have been considering. In the words of the Rev. J. B. Deane, in the Archoeologia Britannica, "The figure of the temple, in almost every religion with which we are acquainted, is the hierogram of its God. The hierogram of the sun was always a circle; the temples of the sun were circular. The Arkites adored the personified Ark of Noah; their temples were built in the form of a ship. The Ophites adored a serpent deity; their temples assumed the form of a serpent. And to come home to our own times and feelings, the Christian retains a remnant of the same idea when he builds his temples in the form of a cross — the cross being at once the symbol of his creed and the hierogram of his God."

3-3 "Graded Way" Near Piketon Ohio

Before leaving inclosures and proceeding to a notice of the mounds and their contents, it will not be out of place to notice a class of ancient works which are of rather an anomalous character, and can hardly be classed under either of these denominations. These are what have been called "Graded Ways," ascending sometimes from one terrace to another, and occasionally toward the banks of rivers or water courses. A fine example is afforded near the town of Piketon, Pike County, Ohio, of which a view is presented in Figure 3. It consists of a graded or artificial inclined ascent from the second to the third terrace—the latter being elevated 17 feet above the former. The way is 1080 feet long by 215 feet wide at one extremity, and 203 feet wide at the other, measuring between the bases of the banks. The earth is thrown outward on either hand, forming embankments, varying on their outer sides, according to the depth of the excavation, from five to eleven feet in height. At the lower extremity of the grade, represented in the engraving, the banks are 22 feet high. The easy ascent this afforded from one terrace to another is made use of practically by the Chilicothe and Portsmouth turnpike which runs through it. The walls are covered with trees and bushes, and hundreds ride between them without suspecting their artificial origin. At first glance it would appear that this work was constructed simply to facilitate ascent from one terrace to another, but it can hardily be supposed that so much labor would have been expended for an object equally well effected with less effort. It has been suggested that the Scioto River once flowed at the foot of the terrace at this point, and that the way led down to it. But the river now flows half a mile to the left, and two terraces, each 20 feet high, intervene between the present and supposed ancient level of the stream. To assent to the suggestion would therefore be to admit an almost immeasurable antiquity for the work in question.

Having treated of "Inclosures for Defense" and "Sacred Inclosures," I now proceed to speak of the other classes of American Antiquities.

## Sepulchral Mounds

[Scattered over the country at irregular intervals, of various sizes from five to one hundred feet in height, in the plains, on eminences, in inclosures; generally of earth, occasionally of stones; containing usually one skeleton, sometimes two, rarely more, buried in a rude chamber of wood or stones, in shallow cists dug beneath the original level of the earth, or simply placed on the original surface of the ground, and covered with bark or matting; frequent evidences of fire in various parts of the mound near its surface, and frequent secondary or recent burials by races subsequent to the builders, who regarded the mounds with a certain degree of veneration.]

3-4 Group of Sepulchral Mounds, Near Chilicothe, Ohio

The most enduring monuments of primeval ages were those erected in memory of the dead; and it seems that the further we go back into man's history of mankind the deeper we find his veneration for his departed brethren. The simplest, and also the most enduring method of preserving the memory of the departed, was by raising a barrow or mound of stones or of earth over his remains; and accordingly we find instances of this mode of interment all over the globe. Even the pyramids of Egypt, now ascertained to have been only just sepulchral monuments, may be regarded as perfected *tumuli*, carrying back the practice to which I have referred far beyond the dawn of written history. In the deep night of ages, step by step, had the rude heap of stones which filial regard first gathered over the dead developed itself, until, in its massive proportions and solid strength, it emulated the mountains and bade defiance to time. Homer speaks frequently of the sepulchral *tumuli* of the Heroic Age of Greece, and gives many curious details connected with interments in them. The description of the burial of Patroclus is familiar to most readers. After the burning of the body, and the performance of various sacrifices, the bones were collected, and the Greeks ordered to raise a *tumulus* over them:

"The Greeks obey!
Where yet the embers glow,
Wide o'er the pile the sable wine they throw,
And deep subsides the ashy heap below.
Next the white bones his sad companions place,
With tears collected, in the golden vase.
The sacred relics to the tent they bore;
The urn a veil of linen covered o'er.
That done, they bid the sepulcher aspire,
And cast the deep foundations round the pyre;
High in the midst they heap the swelling bed
Of rising earth, memorial of the dead."

Again, Hector is made to speak of one whom he is to slay in single combat:

"The long haired Greeks
To him, upon the shores of Hellespont,
A mound shall heap; that those in after times
Who sail along the darksome sea shall say,
'This is the monument of one long since
Borne to his grave, by mighty Hector slain."

The same practice of erecting mounds over the dead prevailed extensively in America, particularly in Peru, where they are called *huacas* and often contain much treasure, and throughout Central America and Mexico. But nowhere are they more numerous or of more imposing size than in the Mississippi Valley. Until within a few years all, or very nearly all, of those in that valley were regarded as places of burial; and the popular idea was that each was a kind of general cemetery, containing the bones of many individuals. Such, however, is not the case. As we have already intimated, a large part of the mounds were connected with the sacred structures which have been described, and dedicated to religious purposes. Those devoted

81

to sepulture generally stand apart from these works, sometimes in groups but usually singly, and are scattered without order over the country. Most are from 6 to 8 feet in height, but sometimes they reach an altitude of from 60 to 90 feet. They invariably cover a skeleton (in very rare instances more than one), which, at the time of its interment, was enveloped in bark or coarse matting, or inclosed in a rude sarcophagus of timber built on the original surface of the ground, or buried in a cist dug in the earth beneath. Burial by fire seems to have been frequently practiced; and urn burial, in which the bones were placed in vessels of pottery, also appears to have prevailed to a considerable extent in the Southern States. With the skeletons in these mounds are found various relics of art, comprising ornaments, utensils, and weapons. A single example will sufficiently illustrate the construction of this class of mounds. Figure 5 is a section of a large mound, of which Figure 4 is a view, standing six miles below Chilicothe, on the left bank of the Scioto River. It is numbered (1) in the "Map of a section of twelve Miles of the Scioto Valley."

3-5 Section of Sepulchral Mound

There are no inclosures nearer than that represented in Figure 5, a mile distant, although there are a number of other mounds of similar character in its immediate vicinity. It is 22 feet high by 90 feet base. The principal excavation was made (as represented by the lighter lines in the section) from the west side, commencing at about one-third of the height of the mound from the top. At 10 feet below the surface occurred a layer of charcoal (a) not far from 10 feet square, and from 2 to 6 inches in thickness, slightly inclined from the horizontal, and lying mostly to the left of the center of the mound. The coal was coarse and clear, and seemed to have been formed by the sudden covering up of the wood while burning, inasmuch as the trunks and branches retained their form, though entirely carbonized. and the earth immediately above as well as below was burned of a reddish color. Below this layer the earth became much more compact and difficult of excavation. At the depth of 22 feet, and on a level with the original surface, immediately underneath the charcoal layer, and, like that, somewhat to one side of the center of the mound, was found a rude timber framework, now reduced to an almost impalpable powder, but the cast of which was still retained in the hard earth. This inclosure of timber, measured from outside to outside, was 9 feet long by 7 wide, and 20 inches high. It had been constructed of logs laid one on the other, and had evidently been covered with other timbers, which had sunk under the superincumbent earth as they decayed. The bottom had also been covered with bark, matting, or thin slabs—at any rate, a whitish stratum of decomposed material remained, covering the bottom of the parallelogram. Within this rude coffin, with its head to the west, was found a human skeleton, or rather the remains of one, for scarcely a fragment as long as one's finger could be recovered. It was so much decayed that it crumbled to powder under the slightest touch. Around the neck of the skeleton, forming a triple row and retaining their position as originally strung and deposited with the dead, were several hundred beads, made of ivory or the tusks of some animal. Several of these still retain their polish, and bear marks which seem to indicate that they were turned in some machine instead of being carved by hand. A few lamina of mica were also discovered, which completed the list of articles found with this skeleton. The feet of the skeleton were nearly in the center of the mound. A drift beyond it developed nothing new, nor was a corresponding layer of charcoal found on the opposite side of the mound. It is clear, therefore, that the *tumulus* was raised over this single skeleton. In the case of a mound of this class opened at Gallipolis, on the Ohio River, the chamber inclosing the skeleton was found just below the original surface, which can always be detected by a strongly marked line and the uniform drab color of the earth beneath it.

The layer of charcoal is not uniformly found in mounds of this class, though it is a feature of frequent occurrence. It would seem to indicate that sacrifices were made for the dead, or that funeral rites of some kind were celebrated. The fire, in every case, was kept burning for a very brief space, as is shown by the lack of ashes and the slight traces of its action left on the adjacent earth. That it was

3-6 Timber
Sarcophagus

suddenly heaped over is also proved by the facts already presented.

Mounds of this, as of every other class, were often disturbed by the modern Indians, who buried in them, and their skeletons are frequently found, but uniformly near the surface, and in positions and under circumstances which easily prevent their being confounded with the original deposits of the mound builders. The skeletons of the latter are always much decayed; so much so indeed that, in the whole course of the writer's investigations, he was able to recover but one entire skull demonstrably belonging to the race of the mounds. In the barrows of England, however, entire and well preserved skeletons are often found of an antiquity dating far beyond the Roman Conquest. And yet in the damp soil and under the humid skies of that country the conditions for their preservation are far less favorable than here, where the climate is comparatively dry, but where we find the skeletons in a much advanced state of decay. If any inference is to be drawn from this circumstance, it is that the mounds of the Mississippi Valley are older than those of England.

From various features discovered in these sepulchral mounds, it has been suggested that sacrifices or ceremonies of some kind, in which fire performed a part, were solemnized above the dead. The general occurrence of a layer of charcoal at some point near the surface of the mound, bearing evidence of having been heaped over while burning, and sometimes having mingled with it human bones, the bones of animals, and relics of art, affords a fair basis for the conjecture.

## Sacred Altar or Sacrificial Mounds

(Almost invariably within sacred inclosures, sometimes conical, curiously stratified throughout their height, with regular altars or basins of burned clay or of stone at their bases, which contain abundant relics of ancient art. In common with the sepulchral mounds they often contain human skeletons of comparatively late deposit. This class also includes the mounds of regular outline, truncated, terraced, ascended by graded ways, of generally vast size, corresponding with the "high places" of the ancients, and the *Teocallis* of Mexico; round, square, rectangular, oval, or octagonal in shape; seldom containing human remains; is some cases probably the bases on which chapels or temples were erected, in other cases used as simple altars on which sacrifices and other religious rites were performed.)

The mounds called, for reasons which will appear as we proceed, altar or sacrificial mounds, are richest in relics of art of any found in the Mississippi Valley, and for this reason most interesting. They occur only within or in the immediate vicinity of inclosures or sacred places; they are stratified, and they contain symmetrical altars of burned clay or stone, on which are found various relics of art and other remains, which in all cases have been more or less subjected to the action of fire. Their characteristics will be best explained by reference to the accompanying section, which may be taken as a type of the whole class, although there are no two precisely alike in all their details. The section is of a mound which occurs in a group of twenty-six, embraced in a single inclosure on the banks of the Scioto River, three miles above the city of Chilicothe. This inclosure is indicated by the letter (E) in the "Map of a Section of twelve Miles of the Scioto Valley." The mound itself is 7 feet high by 55 feet base. A shaft 5 feet square was sunk from its apex, with the following results:

1st. Occurred a layer of coarse gravel and pebbles, which appeared to have been taken from deep pits surrounding the inclosure or from the bank of the river. This layer was one foot in thickness.

2d. Beneath this layer of gravel and pebbles, to the depth of two feet, the earth was homogeneous, though slightly mottled, as if taken up and deposited in small loads from different localities. In one place appeared a deposit of dark colored surface loam, and by its side, or covering it, there was a mass of the clayey soil of greater depth. The outlines of these various deposits could be distinctly traced.

3d. Below this deposit of earth occurred a thin and even layer of fine sand, a little over an inch in thickness.

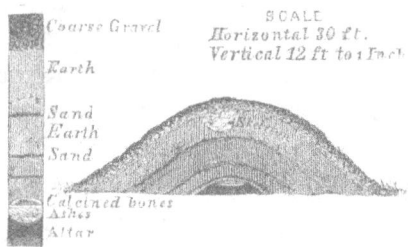

3-7 Section of Sacrificial Mound

4th. A deposit of earth, as above, eighteen inches in depth.

5th. Another stratum of sand, somewhat thinner than the one above mentioned.

6th. Another deposit of earth, one foot thick beneath which was

7th. A third stratum of sand; below which was

8th. Still another layer of earth, a few inches in thickness; which rested on

9th. An altar, or basin, of burned clay.

3-8 Plan and Section
of Alter

This altar was perfectly round. Its form and dimensions are best shown by the supplementary plan and section (Figure 8). (F F) is the altar, measuring, from (c) to (d), nine feet; from (a) to (e), five feet; height from (b) to (e), twenty inches; dip of curve, (a r e), nine inches. The sides, (c a), (e d), slope regularly, at a given angle. The body of the altar is burned throughout, though in a greater degree within the basin, where it was so hard as to resist the blows of a heavy hatchet, the instrument rebounding as if struck upon a rock. The basin, or hollow of the altar, was filled even full with fine dry ashes, intermixed with which were some fragments of pottery, of an excellent finish and elegant model, ornamented with tasteful carvings on the exterior. One of the vases, taken in fragments from this mound, has been very nearly restored. The accompanying sketch (Figure 9) presents its outlines and the character of its ornaments. Its height is six, its greatest diameter eight inches. The material is hardly distinguishable from that composing the pottery of the ancient Peruvians; and in respect to finish, it is fully equal to the best Peruvian specimens. A few convex copper discs, much resembling the bosses used upon harnesses, were also found.

3-9 Vase from the Mounds

Above the deposit of ashes, and covering the entire basin, was a layer of silvery or opaque mica, in sheets, overlapping each other.; and immediately over the center of the basin was heaped a quantity of burned human bones, probably the amount of a single skeleton, in fragments. The position of these is indicated by (o) in the section. The layer of mica and calcined bones, it should be remarked to prevent misapprehension, were peculiar to this individual mound, and were not found in any other of the class.

It will be seen by the section that, at a point about two feet below the surface of the mound, a human skeleton was found. It was placed a little to the left of the center, with the head to the east, and was so much decayed as to render it impossible to extract a single bone entire. Above the skeleton, its shown in the section, the earth and outer layer of gravel and pebbles were broken up and intermixed. Thus, while on one side of the shaft the strata were broken up and confused, on the other they were undisturbed and clearly marked. These circumstances prove conclusively that this skeleton was deposited after the construction of the mound, and doubtless by the Indian races who have succeeded its builders in their occupation of the country. As a general rule, to which there are few exceptions, the only authentic and undoubted remains of the mound builders are found directly beneath the apex of the mound, on a level with the original surface of the earth; and it may be safely assumed that whatever deposits occur near the surface of the mounds are of a date subsequent to their erection. In the class of mounds now under consideration we have data which will admit of no doubt, whereby to judge of the origin, as well as the relative periods, of the various deposits found in them. If the stratification already mentioned as characterizing them is unbroken and undisturbed, if the strata are regular and entire, it is certain that whatever occurs beneath them was placed there at the period of the construction of the mound. And if, on the other hand, these strata are broken up, it is equally certain that the mound has been disturbed and new deposits made since its erection. In this view, the fact of stratification becomes important as well as interesting, for it serves to fix beyond all dispute the origin of many singular relics having a decisive bearing on some of the leading questions connected with American Archeology. The thickness of the exterior layer of gravel in mounds of this class varies, with the dimensions of the mound, from eight to twenty inches. In a very few instances, the layer, which may have been designed to protect the form of the mound, is entirely wanting. The number and relative position of the sand strata are variable; in some of the larger mounds there are as many as six of them, in no case less than one, usually two or three.

Mounds of this class are most fruitful in relics of the builders. On the altars have been found, though much injured and broken up by the action of fire, instruments and ornaments of silver, copper, stone, and bone; beads of silver, copper, pearls, and shell; spear and arrow heads of flint, quartz, garnet, and obsidian; fossil teeth of the shark; teeth of the alligator; marine shells; galena; sculptures of the human head and of numerous animals; pottery of various kinds, and a large number of interesting articles, some of which evince great skill in art, to which allusion will be had further on.

What are called temple mounds may be distinguished by their great regularity of form and general large dimensions. They occur generally within inclosures, but occasionally stand isolated, and consist chiefly of pyramidal structures, truncated, and having graded or winding ascents to their summits. In some instances they are

terraced, or built of successive stages. But whatever their form—
round, oval, octangular, or square—they have invariably level tops
of greater or less area. Some are only a few feet in elevation,
although covering large spaces of ground; such are popularly known
as "platforms." Mounds of this class are not numerous in the Valley
of the Ohio and on the upper tributaries of the Mississippi, but are
numerous in the Southern States, whence we shall draw our present
illustrations.

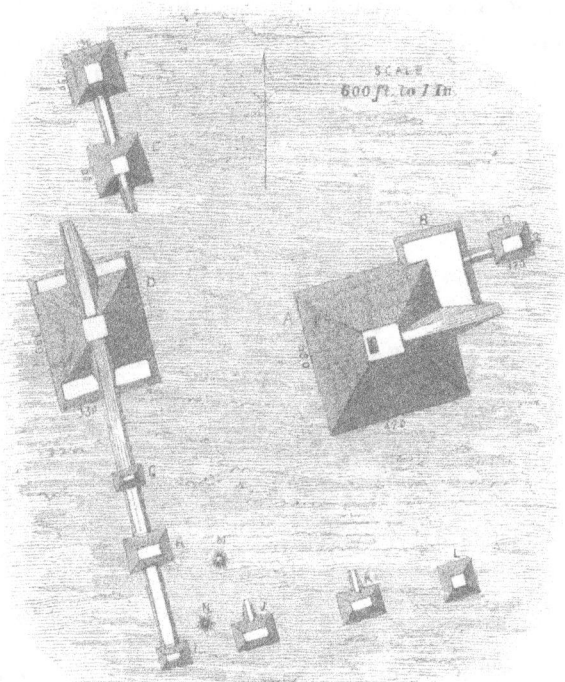

3-10 Ancient Works, Washington County, Mississippi

Figure 10 is a plan of a group of these mounds never before
published. It is found in Washington County, Mississippi, on the road
from the Mississippi River, opposite Point Chicot to William's
Bayou. It will be observed that the group is made up of a series of
rectangular mounds, of various sizes, all truncated, and nearly all
ascended by inclined paths. Several are connected with each other by
raised causeways. The principal mound, (A), is 420 by 390 feet
square at its base, 55 feet high, and has a level area at its summit 120
feet long by 100 feet broad. A graded roadway, 30 feet wide, leads to

89

its top from the east. At its base to the northeastward is a "platform" or raised area, (B), 10 feet high and 75 feet wide, with a small mound, (C), on the right, 120 by 90 feet at the base, with which it is connected by a terrace 4 feet high and 25 feet broad. On the top of the great mound, (A), is an excavation 30 feet long, 25 broad, and 6 deep. A number of smaller rectangular mounds, with graded ascents, form, in conjunction with that just described, and are of nearly equal size to the left, a rectangular inclosure, within which are a few conical mounds. All the mounds of this group are well preserved, and display a wonderful regularity of outline. It is represented that numbers of conical mounds, of different sizes, are scattered over the adjacent country. Deep excavations, from which the earth for the construction of these mounds was obtained, are to be found within a few hundred yards of the group.

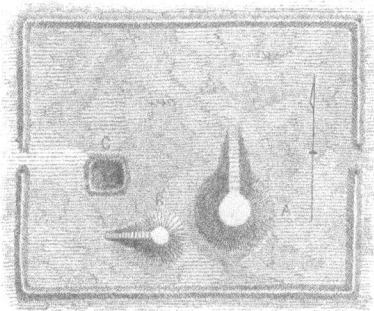

3-11 Ancient Works LaFayette County Miss.

A few miles southeast of Delta, Lafayette County, Mississippi, is a square inclosure, containing two mounds of similar character with those described, of which Figure 11 is a plan.

The inclosure has an area of about 20 acres. The mound, (A), covers an acre of ground, and is 40 feet high. It is truncated, and the level area at its summit is reached by an inclined plane or graded way from the north. (B) is less in size, but of precisely the same form. It is 25 feet in height. (C) is an excavation 15 feet deep and 100 feet in diameter, and is surrounded by a low embankment three feet in height.

Within the ancient works at Marietta, in Ohio, there are a number of temple mounds of great regularity, of one of which Figure 12 is a plan. It is 188 feet long by 132 wide, and 10 feet high. Midway on

90

each side are graded ascents, rendering easy the passage to the area at its summit. These grades are each 25 feet wide and 60 feet long. One of the most remarkable of this class of ancient monuments is the great mound of Cahokia, Illinois, of which an engraving was given in a previous article. Its form is that of a parallelogram, 700 feet long by 500 wide at the base. It is 90 feet high. Upon one side is a broad apron or terrace, which is reached by a graded ascent. At the time this mound was occupied by the Monks of La Trappe the terrace was used as a garden. It is 160 feet wide and 350 long. The summit, or highest part of the mound, measures 200 feet in width by 450 in length. This mound covers not far from eight acres of ground, and the area of its level summit is about five acres. Its solid contents may be roughly estimated at 20,000,000 of cubic feet.

3-12 Temple Mound Marietta Ohio

So far as ascertained these mounds cover no remains, and they were obviously designed as the sites of temples or of other structures which have passed away, or as "high places" for the performance of religious ceremonies. The likeness which they bear to the *Teocallis* of Mexico is striking, and suggestive of their probable purposes.

## Animal Shaped Mounds

(In the form of men, animals, birds, and reptiles; in Ohio on elevated positions; in Wisconsin on level ground, usually open prairies, abundant, and often containing human remains; probably symbolical in their forms, and connected with the religious or totemic systems of the aborigines.]

3-13 Animal Shaped Mounds Wisconsin

It has already been observed that, in the southern portions of the Mississippi Valley, inclosures, whether for defense or other purposes, are comparatively few, while mounds are numerous and of great size and symmetry. Going to the northwest, we also find that inclosures are rare; but the mounds take new and singular forms, almost justifying the belief that they were not built by the same people who constructed those which have been described in the preceding pages. Here they generally assume the form of animals, beasts, birds, and reptiles, and in some cases the outlines of human beings. These effigies are situated on the undulating prairies and level plains, and are accompanied by conical mounds and occasional lines of embankment; but the latter, except in few instances, have no obvious design, and enter into none of those combinations which we observe elsewhere. They are seldom isolated, but occur in groups or ranges, sometimes placed with apparent design in respect to each other. In these groups may be observed every variety of form—the circular, quadrangular, and animal shaped structures occurring in such connections with each other as to justify the belief that they are of contemporaneous origin. At first glance they resemble the ground plans or foundation lines of buildings, and it is not until their entire outline is taken into view that the impression of an effigy becomes decided. This is not surprising, since they are usually of inconsiderable height, varying from one to four feet in height, rarely reaching six feet. Their outlines are, nevertheless, distinctly defined in all cases where they occupy favorable positions. Figure 13 represents a group which occurs in Dane County, Wisconsin, on the great Indian trail or war path from the Mississippi River to Lake Michigan. It consists of six effigies of quadrupeds, six mounds in the form of parallelograms, one effigy, supposed to be of a human figure, one circular tumulus, and one small circle. It is not easy to make out from the effigies what kind of animal is intended to be represented. Perhaps it was the bear; at least they bear a closer resemblance to it than to any other animal with which we are acquainted. These figures vary from 90 to 120 feet in length. The length of the supposed figure of a man, with arms and legs extended, is 125 feet, its width between the points of the arms, 140 feet. The body is 30 feet broad, and its greatest elevation in any part 6 feet. The conical mound in the center of the group is highest, and commands a view of the entire series. For a space of twenty miles around this group similar monuments are to be discovered in every direction and in large numbers. Figures of buffaloes, birds, turtles, lizards, etc., as represented in Figure 14, are common among these remains, the purposes of which remain unexplained. Some of the conical mounds have been found to contain skeletons, as have also some of those in the form of animals. But most of them do not, nor is it clear that the burials which have been found are not secondary deposits. By some they have been regarded as tribal memorials, or a development of the totemic system of the Indians. It is perhaps safest, for the present, to pronounce no other judgment on them than that they are anomabons and unintelligible. It should be mentioned that they are numerous, and that probably several thousands of them occur in the State of Wisconsin alone.

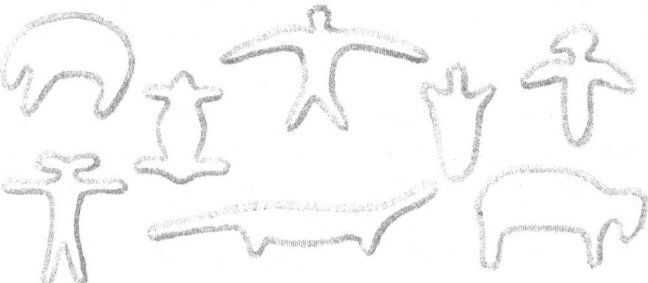

3-14 Forms of Animal Shaped Mounds

94

# Mounds of Observation

3-15 Mounds of Observation

[Lookouts, or sentinels, stations; of variable size; usually in connection with defensive inclosures; destitute of remains.]

Under this denomination I have elsewhere classified those mounds which we find placed on commanding positions in or near works of defense, or on conspicuous points visible from the ancient centers of population, which do not contain human remains, and are therefore not sepulchral; which are not regular in form, like the temple mounds; and which do not contain altars, like those classified as altar mounds.

Some have their summits made up of ashes, coals, and burned materials, indicating that great fires, at some period or other, were kept up on them; and as we know that mounds, in corresponding positions, were often erected as signal or telegraphic stations in the old world, we may infer that these were dedicated to a similar purpose. Nearly every important defensive work has some such mound in or near it, on which we may plausibly conclude sentinels were placed to give notice of the approach of an enemy, or to watch his movements. Some of them may have been used as commanding points whence to harass an assailant; in this respect answering to the purpose of a tower in the medieval systems of fortification. Between Chilicothe and Columbus, on the eastern border of the Scioto Valley, a distance of more than forty miles, a series of mounds may be traced, occupying commanding positions, and so situated in respect to each other that, if the country were cleared of forests, signals of fire might be transmitted in a few minutes along the whole line. As already observed, some of these hill mounds contain human remains, and the reasons for believing that they were primarily, or even secondarily, signal stations, are by no means as numerous or conclusive as in respect to the mounds found in connection with works obviously defensive.

## Implements and Utensils

[Spear and arrow points of stone and copper; stone and copper axes and knives; pottery of various kinds, vases, terra cotta figures, etc.; graving tools of copper; elaborately sculptured pipes; grinding stones; enigmatical tubes and disks; stamps of stone and clay, etc., etc.]

The condition of the ordinary arts of life among the people who constructed the various classes of works which we have described furnishes a prominent and interesting subject of inquiry. As already remarked, the mounds are the principal depositories of ancient art, and in them we must seek for the only authentic remains of the builders. In the observance of a practice almost universal among barbarous or semi-civilized nations, the mound builders deposited various articles of use and ornament with their dead. They also, under the prescriptions of their religion, or in accordance with customs unknown to us, and to which perhaps no direct analogy is afforded by those of any other people, placed upon their altars numerous ornaments and implements—probably those most valued by their possessors—which remain there to this day, attesting at once the religious zeal of the depositors and their skill in the minor arts.

Of course the relics found in the mounds are such only as, from the nature of the materials of which they are composed, have been able to resist the general course of decay, such as articles of pottery, bone, shell, stone, and metal. We can expect to find but slight traces of instruments or utensils of wood, and but few and doubtful ones of the materials which went to compose articles of dress. The only metal found in any degree of abundance in the mounds is copper.

In Figure 16 is a sketch of a copper axe, found in a mound near Chilicothe, Ohio. It is solid and well hammered, and weighs two pounds five ounces. It is seven inches long by four broad at the cutting edge, and has an average thickness of little less than four-tenths of an inch. Its edge is slightly curved, somewhat after the manner of the axes of the present day, and is beveled from both surfaces. Copper chisels, gravers, etc., have also been found in the mounds, of which Figure 17 represents some specimens, the largest of which is eight inches long. The metal seems, however, to have been more generally applied to ornamental than useful purposes; for, while articles of ornament are common in both the sacrificial and sepulchral mounds, copper implements are comparatively rare. It is possible that ornaments were more generally placed in the mounds than articles of use; such certainly is the case in respect to the mounds of sepulture.

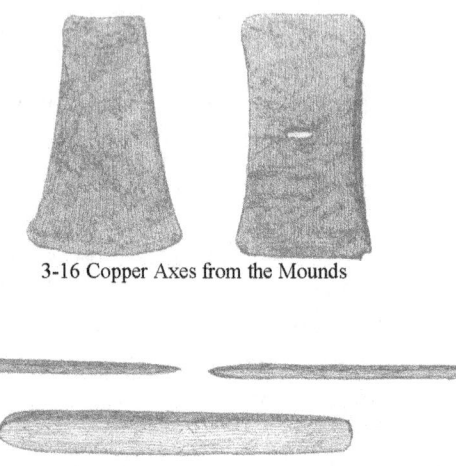

3-16 Copper Axes from the Mounds

3-17 Copper Implements

Silver has also been found, but in small quantities, reduced to great thinness, and closely wrapped around copper ornaments. The ore of lead, galena, has been found in considerable abundance, and some of the metal itself, under circumstances implying a knowledge of its use on the part of the ancient people. The discovery of gold has been vaguely announced, but is not well attested. It is not impossible that articles of that metal have been found, with other vestiges of European art, accompanying secondary and recent deposits, which are often confounded with those of the mound builders by ignorant or credulous explorers. No iron, or traces of iron, have yet been discovered, except in connection with recent deposits. There are many good reasons for believing that both the silver and copper found in the mounds were obtained from the mineral regions of Lake Superior, where, it is well known, there are abundant traces of ancient mining. The articles composed of these metals are without alloy, and appear to have been worked from the native masses.

Arrow and lance heads, and cutting instruments of the numerous varieties of quartz, embracing every shade of color and degree of transparency, from the dull blue of the ordinary horn stone to the brilliant opalescence of the chalcedonic varieties, are frequent in the mounds. Some are worked with exquisite skill from pure, limpid crystals of quartz; others from crystals of manganesian garnet; and others still from obsidian. It is a singular fact, however, that none of these, nor indeed any traces of weapons, have been discovered in the "sepulchral mounds;" most of the remains found with the skeletons being evidently such as were deemed ornamental, or recognized as badges of distinction. Some of the altar or sacrificial mounds, on the other hand, have the deposits within them almost entirely made up of finished arrow and spear points, intermixed with masses of the unmanufactured material. From one altar were taken several bushels of finely worked lance heads of milky quartz, nearly all of which had been broken up by the action of fire. In another mound an excavation six feet long and four broad disclosed upward of six hundred spearheads or disks of hornstone, rudely blocked out, and the deposit extended indefinitely on every side.

3-18 Vase from the Mounds

In the manufacture of pottery the mound builders attained a considerable proficiency. Many of the vases recovered from the mounds display, in respect to material, finish, and model, a marked superiority to any thing of which the existing Indian tribes are known to have been capable, and compare favorably with the best Peruvian specimens. Though of great symmetry of proportions, there is no good reason to believe that they were turned on a lathe. Their fine finish seems to have been the result of the same process with that adopted by the Peruvians in their manufactures. Some of them

99

are tastefully ornamented with scrolls, figures of birds, and other devices, which are engraved in the surface, instead of being embossed upon it. The lines appear to have been cut with some sharp, gouge shaped instrument, which entirely removed the detached material, leaving no ragged or raised edges. Nothing can exceed the regularity and precision with which the ornaments are executed. The material of which the vases are composed is a fine clay, which, in the more delicate specimens, was worked nearly pure, or possessing a very slight silicious intermixture. Some of the coarser specimens have pulverized quartz mingled with the clay; while others are tempered with salmon colored mica, in small flakes, which gives them a ruddy and rather brilliant appearance, and was, perhaps, introduced with some view to ornament as well as utility. None appear to have been glazed; though one or two, either from baking or the subsequent great heat to which they were subjected, exhibit a slightly vitrified surface. Figure 18 is a good example of the form and style of the vases recovered. It was taken from a mound in "Mound City," in fragments, but subsequently restored. Its height is five and a half, and its diameter six and a half inches. The thickness of the vase is about one-sixth of an inch, and uniform throughout. It is of a dark brown color; its surface smooth, and of an unctuous feel. Terra cottas, representing animals, etc., are not unfrequently found in the mounds, but are less numerous than those of stone. Many of the latter display great taste and skill, a close observance of nature, and a minutes attention to details. None, however, obviously designed as idols or objects of worship have been taken from the mounds. Most, in fact, are what may be called ornamented pipes, wrought in a multitude of characteristic representations of the human head, animals, birds, etc., of which they give to a surprising degree the characteristic attitudes and expression. Of those of the human head Figure 19 may be taken as a fair example. It is engraved of full size. The material is a fine grained, compact stone, much altered in color and other respects from the action of fire. The muscles of the face are well exhibited,, and the forehead is finely molded. The eyes are prominent and open, and the lips full and rounded. The knots observable at the top of the forehead and just back of the ears may be designed to represent the manner in which the hair was gathered or wound. It appears reasonable to suppose that this, and the other sculptured heads found in the mounds, were copied from nature, and display the characteristic features of the ancient race.

3-19 Sculpure of the Human Head

3-20 Sculpted Bird from the Mounds

Figure 20 is a good example of the carvings in representation of birds and animals. It is the figure of some rapacious bird, probably some variety of the hawk or eagle, in the act of tearing in pieces a small bird, which it grasps in its claws. The workmanship is spirited and lifelike, as well as minute and delicate. The wings are folded across each other, and the finer feathers on their superior portions, as well as on the thighs, are well represented. The eyes were composed of small pearls. In fact, pearls were inserted for eyes in all the sculptures of birds. The material of this pipe is a hard, red porphyry. Other sculptures represent an otter with a fish in his mouth, a heron devouring a fish; others still, bears, beavers, panthers, the elk, the squirrel, the opossum, the frog, toad, swallow, duck, buzzard, rattlesnake, etc., etc., all so well executed as to be recognized by the most inexperienced eye at the first glance. Besides these, there are carvings of various birds and animals not indigenous to this latitude —such as the toucan, and the lamantin or manitus—of which latter only a few examples have been found in the United States, in the extreme southern parts of Florida. It may be remarked that the mound builders seem to have been inveterate smokers, and that in the construction and ornament of their pipes they displayed their utmost skill. They are always carved from a single piece, and consist of a flat, curved base, of variable length and width, the bowl rising from the convex side. From one of the ends, communicating with the bowl, is drilled a small hole answering the purposes of a tube; the corresponding opposite division being left for the manifest purpose of holding the implement to the mouth.

## Ornaments Etc.

(Beads of pearl, shell, stone, and metal; bracelets of copper; pendants and gorgets of stone, shells, and copper; bosses of metal; teeth of animals, drilled for necklaces; carved rode of bone or ivory, etc., etc.)

A large portion of the articles found in the mounds may he classified as ornaments. Beads are found in the greatest abundance. They may be counted, in some instances, by hundreds and thousands —each one of them the result of no inconsiderable amount of labor, unless we underestimate the means at the command of their makers. Some of them are made of shell, carefully wrapped round or plated over with thin slips of silver. Others are of simple shell worked in every variety of shape, round, oblong, and flattened; others of animal bones and tusks; and many of pearls and small marine shells. The perforated teeth of the wildcat, wolf, and shark, as well as the claws of animals, and sections of the bones of birds, were used in like manner. The beads of bone often retain their polish. They resemble sections cut from the ends of small cylinders, and subsequently more or less rounded on their edges and perforated,, and resemble the bone buttons of commerce. The pearl beads are simply perforated pearls, some of which must have been of great size and value, obtained from the freshwater shells, or *unios* of the Western rivers. No less than two quarts of these, burned and no longer of value, were obtained from a single mound.

3-21 Beads from the Mounds

3-22 Copper Bracelets

Bracelets of copper, of which Figure 22 illustrates the universal character, are also often found in the mounds, usually encircling the arms of skeletons. But they are not uncommon in the altar mounds. They consist of a small rod of copper, hammered out with more or less skill, and so bent that the ends approach or lap over each other. Some of them are exceedingly well and smoothly wrought. A kind of copper gorget or plate, apparently to be worn on the breast, is occasionally found. Figure 23 is an example. The original is eight and a half inches in greatest length, and four and a quarter inches broad, perforated with two holes near its upper edge. A large number of disks or medals of copper, which, to use a familiar illustration, resemble the bosses used on harnesses. Some of them are not less than ten inches in diameter. They are formed of thin plates of copper, are perfectly round and concave-convex in shape. Figure 24 is an example of this kind of disk, and represents also two specimens of a smaller variety of boss or button. These present a convex and plane surface, and are identical in shape with the old fashioned buttons which linger on the small clothes of our grandfathers. They are hollow. Some are perforated from their sides, but most have the holes through which passed the thread or thong for attaching them to any object in their base.

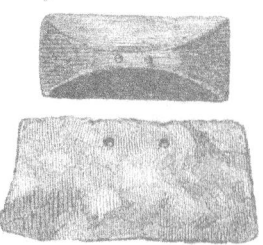

3-23 Copper Gorget

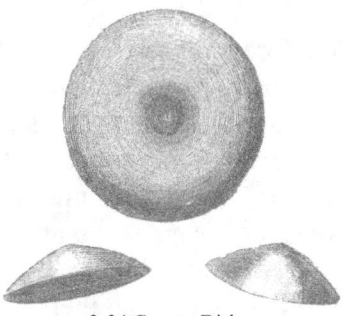

3-24 Copper Disks

Examples of ornaments and other relics from the mounds might be almost indefinitely extended; but a notice of them would far transcend the limits of an article like this, which at best can only aim to give a very general outline of their character. Many of them are of a very interesting character, not less from illustrating the state of ancient art, than as enabling us, from the material of which they are composed, their peculiarities of form, and correspondences of use, to define the intercourse, and, in some degree, the connections, of the ancient races. From what has already been presented, it will be seen that there are gathered in the mounds, or the alluvions of the Ohio, copper and silver from the Great Lakes; pearls and shells from the Southern Gulf; mica from the primitive ranges of the Alleghenies, and obsidian from the volcanic ridges of Mexico—an extended range, the extremes of which define, with great precision, the field in which the mounds occur. It would almost seem that the ancient race existed contemporaneously over this great area, maintaining throughout a constant intercourse.

## General Deductions

After a perusal of the foregoing accounts of the military works, the sacred inclosures, pyramidal structures, and remains of art of the ancient people who once occupied the Mississippi Valley, and have left only these monuments to record the fact of their existence, the reader will naturally inquire, "Who were this ancient people? When did they live? Why have they disappeared, and whither have they gone?" But these are questions more easily asked than answered. As already said, history is mute concerning them, and their very name is lost to tradition. We only know that they must have been a numerous, stationary, and agricultural people; for a nomadic population would never rear works so extensive, systematic, and manifestly of permanent intention; and a population so large as to afford the labor for their construction could not subsist on the precarious and scanty returns of the chase. And if the mound builders were a numerous, stationary, and agricultural people, it follows almost of necessity that their customs, laws, and religion had assumed a fixed and well defined form. If we are not mistaken in our own conclusions as to the character of a large portion of the most imposing remains of the ancient people, their superstitions and religious notions must have coincided very nearly with those of the primitive nations of the old world, and have exercised a strong, if not a controlling influence on their character. That they had extensive intercourse, by means of exchange with other tribes or otherwise, is shown from the variety of remains found in the mounds of remote origin, and which must have been brought to their places of final deposit from great distances. That they had some standard of measurement seems probable from the circumstances of their reproducing great works of exactly coinciding dimensions in localities remote from each other. That they were not deficient in notions of geometrical accuracy is abundantly shown by the number of perfect geometrical figures which they have left embossed on the face of the country. That they were close observers of nature and natural objects is shown from the fidelity with which, they reproduced, in the most obdurate materials, the figures of men and animals. Their refinement in taste is shown in the graceful forms and ornamentation of their pottery. In all these respects their works show them to have been far in advance of the tribes found in occupation of the country at the time of the Discovery. But there is no evidence that their condition was any thing more than an approximation to that attained by the ancient Mexicans, Central Americans, and Peruvians. They did not possess, like these, the art of working in metals; nor is there the slightest authentic evidence that they made any approach whatever to the hieroglyphic system or systems of representation which were practiced by the latter, with more or less of success, in the recording of events and the transmission of ideas. Stories of the alleged discovery in the mounds of tablets and stones inscribed with letters or hieroglyphic characters may serve to delude fanatics like the Mormons, or engage antiquarians like Jonathan Oldbuck, but they are beneath notice or criticism on the part of intelligent students of archeology.

As regards the antiquity of the works of the Mississippi Valley, nothing can be affirmed with exactness. That many of them are very ancient, dating back by thousands of years, seems to be fairly deducible from a variety of circumstances. Not only are they covered by primitive forests of trees, some of which have an antiquity of from six to eight hundred years; but even these forests appear to stand on the debris of others equally venerable, which preceded them, since the era of the mounds. Numerous works exist, in part cut away by the action of rivers which have since changed their courses and receded to distances of half a mile or more, the intervening ground having since become covered with heavy forests, apparently the successors of others on the same ground. It is impossible to say how long a period such physical changes would require; but we are safe in estimating it by centuries. The extreme decay of the skeletons in the mounds, and the depth of vegetable mold accumulated in the trenches of the ancient works, are also important circumstances bearing on the antiquity of these monuments, and indicate a very great age.

Whether the race of the mounds disappeared under some sudden or overwhelming irruption of hostile nations, were swept away by some devastating epidemic, like those which Mexican tradition records, or migrated elsewhere under the pressure of powerful neighbors or under the seductions of a more genial climate, are questions of deep interest, but to which we can, as yet, give no satisfactory answer.